Economic Dimensions
in Education

Economic Dimensions in Education

Martin O'Donoghue

Fellow of Trinity College, Dublin

ALDINE · ATHERTON
CHICAGO · NEW YORK

First U.S. edition published 1971 by
Aldine · Atherton, Inc.
529 South Wabash Avenue
Chicago, Illinois 60605

Library of Congress Catalog Card Number 79–133246
ISBN 202–06038–1

Printed and bound in the Republic of Ireland
by Cahill and Co. Limited, Dublin

Contents

Preface

A BOOK which is devoted to the economic aspects of an industry must inevitably, among other issues, deal with the question of efficiency. In the case of education, which results in multiple outputs of a kind not readily measurable in monetary terms, one essential prerequisite for any satisfactory assessment of efficiency is an adequate statement of the objectives which each programme or activity is designed to achieve.

Equity would appear to require that the same approach be applied to this book. My intention is that it should provide an exposition of the economic approach to educational issues in a manner calculated to require the least cost, in terms of time and effort, on the part of the three groups for whom it is primarily intended! The first of these is economics students, whether at graduate or undergraduate level, who are interested in social economics, public expenditure analysis or related areas. The second is students of the social sciences whose primary interest may lie elsewhere, but who require an understanding of the economic issues in education. The third group comprises those educators, administrators and others who, in their professional capacities, find themselves frequently confronted with economic problems or constraints on education. In addition to these groups, I would not exclude the possibility that the book may be of interest to others, especially that nebulous group, 'the intelligent laymen', who take an active interest in so many topics.

Seeking to cater for these somewhat diverse groups poses some problems of exposition. Mathematical formulations have been avoided and there is a minimum use of diagrams and economic 'jargon'. At the same time I have sought to ensure that the exposition is sufficiently rigorous and comprehensive to be acceptable to the more professional reader. The second problem of exposition was attempting to ensure that there would be a balanced presentation of the frequently divergent viewpoints—not an easy task in an area where there is a high incidence of partisan pleading.

Although I have sought to minimise the intrusion of my own views, since they are inappropriate in a book of this nature, I would expect that this is an objective where only limited success can be expected, given the highly subjective judgements required on both mine and the readers' parts.

My interest in this area began in 1962, when I found myself a member of a team commissioned to study the Irish educational system, as part of a programme involving the majority of O.E.C.D. member countries. So many people have contributed to the formation of my views since then, that it would be a well-nigh impossible task to list those to whom I am indebted. It includes members of the O.E.C.D. staff in the Directorate of Scientific Affairs, as well as colleagues on the national teams in Austria, Germany, Netherlands, Norway, and representatives from the U.S. and U.K. I should add that the indebtedness is not solely intellectual: it extends also to liberal hospitality and numerous friendships. Among my academic debts I am conscious that there are some which require specific mention. Professors Peacock and Wiseman of York University provided their unique blend of camaraderie, stimulation and intellectual discipline at several key points. Professor Patrick Lynch of University College, Dublin, and my colleague, Professor W. J. L. Ryan, are responsible not only for the initial opportunities given to me, but for continuous advice and guidance. The responsibility for the various sins of omission and commission is, of course, mine.

Martin O'Donoghue,
Trinity College, Dublin.

CHAPTER 1

THE ECONOMIC APPROACH TO EDUCATION

THERE has been a growing interest in the economic aspects of education during the past decade. Various reasons can be, and have been, advanced to account for this development. One is the considerable growth in the volume of educational activity to the point where today education is one of the largest industries in most countries and also one of the chief employers of highly skilled personnel. A second is the recognition that education may have a significant influence on the employment and income opportunities open to people and hence affect the distribution of income and wealth in society. A third reason stems from the post-war emphasis on economic growth and development, with education playing an important role as the provider of skilled personnel for an economy.

It is not necessary to continue with any careful cataloguing of such reasons in order to justify the contemporary economic interest in educational activities. A more interesting question is rather to explain the comparative neglect of education by economists in the earlier decades of this century. Studies of, or references to, education by economists in the period are few and far between, in contrast to the many studies of other industries and sectors of the economy.

One possible explanation for this neglect was the absence of a satisfactory analytical framework within which to conduct an economic analysis of education. The accepted framework for analysis of individual sectors was that of the competitive market economy. In this system it is held that competition among buyers and sellers will result in the most efficient pattern of production and consumption for any commodity.

This is so because buyers will only pay prices which do not exceed the value they place on the item in question, while sellers, for their part, will not accept (or not for long) prices which do not cover the costs of supplying the item. In this system over-production would not occur because suppliers would quickly find that they could not dispose of the surplus at a remunerative price. Equally, under-production would not long persist because any scarcity would cause buyers to offer higher prices which would encourage increased supply.

What was true for one item applied equally to all. Competition would determine the correct quantity and price for all the goods and services available in an economy. In this process of determining how the economy's resources would be allocated among various uses, the competitive system would also produce the economically appropriate pattern of income distribution. The income which any individual commanded would be determined by the value of the economic services which he provided. In this way a self-contained economically interdependent system of production and consumption would emerge.

Given this competitive model as the analytical basis, the normal pattern for the study of any one industry or sector would be to examine demand and supply patterns, the development of the industry, its relationship with other industries, and other points of interest in terms of whether they resulted in an adequate degree of competition, and, if not, to identify imperfections in the competitive system with a view to eliminating them.

It is possible to analyse education in a similar manner. One could explore such questions as whether parents/pupils had an adequate knowledge of the costs and quality of the education provided by various schools, whether there was an adequate range of educational establishments available to pupils, whether there was freedom of entry for those seeking to open new schools, and so forth, in the same way as one might look at the shoe, ship or sealing-wax industries. However, it is only necessary to state this type of approach to become aware that this is not the way in which education is customarily described. Education deals with people, and there is a certain distaste in describing educational processes in terms similar to those used for processing animals, vegetables and minerals.

Apart from this aversion to the usual theoretical framework, there is a major practical objection to it on the grounds that the bulk of education in almost all countries is not bought and sold on a competitive market basis, but is rather financed or operated by both governmental and philanthropic agencies.

To discuss education in economic terms, a framework is needed which is appropriate to this pattern of mixed public and private activity which may contain both competitive and philanthropic elements. No adequate framework existed, nor for that matter has one yet emerged. The post-war years, however, did bring a growing interest in, and understanding of, the economic aspects of such mixed situations. In contrast to the earlier position in which taxation, for example, might be extensively discussed, but government spending either ignored or quickly glossed over, there is now considerable economic literature on public sector spending and activities. It is this development which has facilitated the economic treatment of individual expenditure areas, such as education.

But while there have been considerable advances in the treatment and understanding of these areas, there is still no comprehensive theory of public expenditure which could be used as a basis for discussion. Instead there has been a piece-meal type of development with the emphasis on identifying the various causes for intervention with market activities and then attempting to work out the most appropriate methods for the treatment of these problem areas. Since this is also the procedure which will be adopted here, it will be convenient first to summarise and illustrate the manner in which this piecemeal approach has been developed, both in the general case and in the specific area of education.

II

A variety of both non-economic and economic reasons was gradually established which might explain non-competitive types of economic activity. Intervention on non-economic grounds might be prompted by a number of considerations. Thus on humanitarian grounds, a modification of the pattern of incomes produced by a competitive economic system might be sought, because competition is consistent with zero incomes being earned by persons who provide no economic services to the community, such as the sick or the aged. Rather than leave the relief of the resulting distress to private initiative, many economies sanctioned the introduction of taxation policies aimed at redistributing income. Modifications of the competitive pattern of resource-allocation have also been sought on political grounds. The competitive system may call for the importation of foodstuffs or other essential items. For security reasons it may be desired to have such items home-produced, which is frequently achieved by farming subsidies or controls regulating farm output. This list of examples could be lengthened to illustrate the point that in most societies the normal competitive system may be modified because of a conflict between economic and other motivations. While a Marxist might deny the validity of these non-economic motivations, most economists accept that economic man is a fiction (of non-economists), and recognise that many forms of governmental activity will arise from this conflict.

On economic grounds intervention in the competitive system may arise for several reasons. One is that the technical characteristics of a particular industry may be such that a monopoly is the cheapest, or most appropriate, form of supply —telephones, electricity, gas and water, are common examples of a single supply source. Here it would be economically inefficient to maintain or promote competition; instead the monopoly situation is generally accepted and the object is then to devise an appropriate basis for its regulation. These monopolistic situations may also arise, not through any technical factor, but because of human deviations from the requirements of the perfectly competitive model. Thus there may be an inadequate degree of knowledge which prevents potential buyers or sellers from maximising their situation; or there may be restrictions on entry to an industry or occupation which prevent people from acting in accordance with their economic knowledge. In such cases, non-market action may again be advocated to cope with the specific form which these monopolistic situations may take.

A second type of economic problem within the competitive system occurs with items which involve joint consumption, where the exclusion of any one individual or group from sharing in the consumption of the item is either difficult or impossible. The provision of an army or other components of national defence is a standard example of this type of 'public good' problem. Since some of the citizens cannot be excluded from the defence protection provided, it will not be possible to discover how much each individual would freely pay for this service, hence a competitive solution is not feasible.

A third problem arises where the market is not sufficiently comprehensive to embrace all activities involving economic costs and benefits, and where in consequence some resources or outputs are unpriced. This leads to what is termed a divergence between the private and social valuation of the items involved. Standard examples are the effluent discharge from a factory which pollutes a river, killing the fish and spoiling bathing facilities, or the smoke from the factory chimney which soils the laundry in the neighbourhood. Here costs are imposed on anglers, bathers and housewives, as a result of the factory's activities, but these costs are not charged to the factory and hence are not reflected in the prices of its products. The problem in these divergence cases tends to centre around the absence or inadequacy of property rights—whether the anglers have a right to the fishing, the bathers to clean water, the housewives to clean air, or whether the factory has the right to impose these costs. These divergence questions may then be resolved via the legal system, or by taxes/payments to the affected parties.

A special form of this divergence problem which is relevant to investment-type decision may be noted separately. This is the case of the divergence between the private and social valuation of present and future goods. Here the divergence arises because the life expectancy for any individual is both shorter and more uncertain than for the community as a whole; hence individuals will place a relatively higher value on present rather than on future goods. This divergence can be significant if one is interested in questions of economic growth and development, because the volume of saving, and hence of investment, resulting from a free market system will be less than that which would arise from community valuations.

Finally it may be worth noting that if intervention in the competitive system is called for on economic grounds, then there is also a case for intervening to alter the distribution of income and wealth on similar grounds. This is so because the prevailing distribution will no longer reflect an economically 'efficient' pattern of activity. Thus a person might become wealthy, not because he had provided very valuable services to the economy, but because he had enjoyed a monopoly position, or had access to unpaid factors of production.

Similar reasoning may also be applied in seeking to explain the absence of competitive activity in education. First it may be noted that education is a service which is demanded by substantial numbers of consumers; there is rarely, therefore, any monopolistic problem on the demand side. The supply side is, however, less clear-cut and varies both with the level of education and with the particular area under review. Thus in the urban areas of developed countries there is usually a sufficient number of suppliers (schools) at the primary and post-primary levels of education to ensure a reasonable degree of competition. At the higher levels, however, the choice is typically much more restricted; most cities would have only one university for example—hence a significant degree of local monopoly may occur. Similar monopolistic situations will tend to arise in varying degrees in rural areas of developed economies, and in both urban and rural areas of underdeveloped countries for first and second level education. The presence of these monopolistic tendencies may thus constitute one reason for the absence of an adequate market in education.

A second possibility is that education is an activity which gives rise to significant divergences between the private and social valuation of its costs and/or benefits. This is a possibility frequently discussed in the literature on the subject. There are many references to the benefits which the presence of an educated person or group may confer on other sectors of the community. It has been suggested, for example, that educated people may raise the productivity of others with whom they work; that they may lead to reductions in lawlessness and to greater social cohesion and stability; or that they may make democratic political processes possible. These examples all refer to external benefits from education; equally there might be cases where costs might be imposed by educated people on the rest of the economy. Education might, for example, produce discontented intellectuals who would generate social strife, or who would decline to accept 'inferior' employment. Whether beneficial or detrimental, however, the presence of these effects may constitute a second reason for public sector educational activity.

Distribution aspects may be a further factor in such intervention. Governments pursuing policies of income redistribution would presumably be interested in dealing with the causes of unacceptable inequalities. If it could be shown that education is a significant factor in causing income differentials, policies aimed at providing some more widespread pattern of educational opportunities might be pursued as part of any long-term dynamic solution to such distributional problems.

Finally, it may be necessary to take account of the non-economic reasons motivating public sector intervention. Historically it would appear that these were more important than the purely economic factors in many countries. Such viewpoints find expression in references to education as being a desirable thing in itself, as providing its own justification and satisfaction, as an inalienable human right, and so forth. From the introduction of universal compulsory education in nineteenth-century Europe and America to the United Nations charter, the tone in which education is frequently described suggests that it is these non-economic considerations which have been paramount.

III

Elaborating the variety of reasons which can lead to non-competitive forms of economic activity illustrates the complexity of motivation that is possible. In this respect education is not unique since similar complexities arise in many other areas. One purpose which economists have in seeking to identify the various forces at work in any given area is to help in arriving at an adequate description and understanding of them. While positive knowledge of this type is important and valuable in its own right, there is also a second objective in these efforts. This consists in the more difficult and more far-reaching attempt at formulating policy prescriptions and drawing normative conclusions. The temptation to indulge in activities of these latter types in understandable: the areas under investigation utilise large amounts of available resources and they profoundly affect the whole well-being of the population. Since decisions must continually be taken on the size and composition of activity in each area, it is perhaps inevitable that economists seek to make their contribution to such policy-making.

But again in this normative prescriptive sphere there have been significant changes and developments in recent decades. The overwhelming bulk of the prescriptive statements in earlier periods were based on an advocacy of the competitive market system. Competition was good, monopoly bad; free trade between countries was good, restrictions bad. Similarly, increases in government budgets were bad, reductions good—in economics as in other spheres that government was best which governed least. But gradually, as the various problem areas associated with a competitive system were identified, there was a wider recognition and acceptance of the necessity for intervention with the market economy. For a time, indeed, in the post-war period there was a tendency to look on government activity as being more or less automatically justified in all cases where competitive failures were identified. The more recent tendency has been to retreat from each extreme, and to adopt a much more agnostic attitude to the derivation of policy prescriptions and normative statements.

Thus the earlier approach to the 'public good' problems noted above (defence etc.) was to assume that since these items could not be organised competitively, they should be provided through the public sector. The present position is the more cautious one that if the 'ideal' competitive world is not available, it is necessary to examine and compare the various 'second best' positions which may be possible in reality. A careful analysis will normally be needed in order to determine whether private operation or financing would provide a more satisfactory (albeit less than ideal) position than some public sector arrangement. The empirical answer to this question will, moreover, shift from time to time. Technological developments, for example, might mean that it would be feasible to charge vehicles on an individual basis for their use of city streets by fitting some monitoring device, whereas on practical grounds such individual pricing has not hitherto been possible. Again radio and TV signals which have been available to all possessing the necessary receivers could in future be supplied on a selective basis by transmitting 'scrambled' signals which could then be 'decoded' by those who pay for the necessary equipment.

Despite this greater caution, and increased awareness of the limited validity which any prescriptive statements may possess, the practical pressures are such that policy conclusions will continue to be drawn from economic analyses. It will become evident that in this respect too, education has received a similar treatment to that accorded other activities. In this respect, indeed, it might well be contended that education has had more than a fair share of such treatment. Given the importance attached to education by various groups, its ideological and philosophical connotations, the historical controversies which have surrounded so many of its aspects, the opportunities it provides for imposing particular value-systems and thought-patterns on the young, and the emotional reactions which discussions of it can evoke, it would be surprising if economists could avoid the temptation to derive normative/ prescriptive statements from their studies.

The foregoing remarks are intended as a preparation and an apology to the reader for the rather laborious and painstaking treatment of the later chapters. Given the absence of a fully coherent and acknowledged theoretical framework on the one hand, and the temptation to derive policy-relevant statements on the other, it would be all too easy to present particular viewpoints or value-judgements as though they were the result of some objective analysis.

CHAPTER 2

THE DEMAND FOR EDUCATION

In this, and in the three succeeding chapters, the demand aspects of education will be examined. The present chapter will be primarily concerned with such general questions as the total expenditure on education, the trends in these totals, and the factors which appear to influence the level of demand.

The first problem to be resolved is the content and coverage of education for purposes of this discussion. The solution adopted for almost all economic studies, and the one which will be followed here, is to confine attention to the services provided by certain types of establishment, usually schools and colleges. Some of the limitations and dangers of such an approach will be immediately apparent. The more usual way of defining education is in terms of a process, in this case the process by which personality-development takes place. On this definition, by no means all—indeed not necessarily even the major part—of education may take place in educational establishments; the home, work and leisure activities, may each provide educational environments and experiences. In restricting the focus to educational establishments, it is clear that much educational activity will be excluded from the study.

The main reason for adopting this more restricted approach is a practical one. Since no direct measurement of the educational process itself is, as yet, available, any attempt at a comprehensive treatment could result in purely qualitative statements. Economists, however, are primarily interested in quantitative results, and consequently seek measurements of the phenomena which they investigate. This emphasis on measurable phenomena arises from the nature of economics itself, which is concerned with the manner in which choices concerning the use of scarce resources are made. Emphasis on measurement does not, however, entirely preclude the possibility of or necessity for qualitative statements, since appropriate data will not always be available.

While the desire to concentrate on the quantifiable section of educational activity is readily explicable, it must still be asked whether the exclusion of non-school education would not produce results which would be so restricted as to be positively misleading. On this aspect there are two points to be made. One concerns the manner in which the level of educational activity in each sphere is determined. In the case of schools or other educational establishments the volume of activity is presumably motivated primarily by educational considerations —the numbers of schools built, and of teachers and equipment provided, are a reflection of the numbers of pupils to be educated. If pupil numbers grow, so also does the amount of these educational facilities. In contrast, the educational effects of the home, factory, holiday and so forth, are a by-product of activities which are primarily motivated by other objectives. Management decisions concerning the scale or nature of a factory's activities, for example, will rarely take account of the educational consequences which these may have on employees. The home constitutes a more difficult case. Parents may take into account the likely educational effects on their children when deciding their own activities, so that education could be an influence on the pattern of domestic activity. Given our inadequate understanding of human behaviour, however, it seems simpler to treat decisions as to the type of home to be established, whether the mother will work or remain at home, the encouragement or disapproval given to children's activities by parents, and similar home-related questions, as being the outcome of a complex set of motives. The resulting pattern of home activities will yield a certain amount of educational activity, an amount which may be treated as given for our purposes. A similar treatment can be accorded to the educational consequences of church attendance, holiday travel, cinema visits, television viewing, leisure reading, and the myriad of activities all of which may have some educational motivation but whose total volume is unlikely to be significantly affected by changes in their educational side-effects.

The second point by way of justifying the exclusion of non-school education is that economists are not alone in seeking quantifiable phenomena; measurability is applied to education also and has resulted in school-education being treated in practice as something which differs from other educational forms, even though the process itself might be similar. The measures themselves do not deal with education as such, but rather with some component of it, such as the possession of a certain vocabulary, the ability to carry out numerical operations, or more specialised aspects, such as knowledge of the legal system, engineering techniques or so forth. The various certificates, diplomas or degrees, which testify to this possession of the stated level of proficiency in practice constitute items of such value as to mark out institutionalised education as something different from other educational forms. These differences manifest themselves in various ways. In the area of employment, for example, possession of some stipulated qualifications may be necessary in order to obtain various posts, and the qualifications need not always have a direct bearing on the work involved. While, for example, on the one hand it is essential for doctors or lawyers to have the appropriate professional certificates in order to practise, it is equally customary for higher grades in the civil service in some countries to be recruited from among university honours graduates, who may have been students of ancient languages, or similar subjects unconnected with their work. The rationale in stipulating these various qualifications is fairly obvious in the former cases. The patient will feel somewhat happier if he knows that the operating knife is being wielded by someone who has a proven familiarity with human anatomy; likewise the prisoner will prefer an advocate who can defend his cause to the maximum extent of the law. In the civil service case the rationale in stipulating certain qualifications may not, as in the doctor/lawyer examples, lay emphasis on knowledge as such, but may be designed to identify persons with proven levels of intellectual ability, capacity for personal initiative, or whatever attributes may be deemed to be associated with success in academic studies.

These examples suggest that the qualifications provided by

educational institutions, though they do not measure education as normally defined, serve a valuable purpose which distinguishes these institutions from other forms of education, and the difference is sufficiently great as to make their graduates the products of a separate industry. There is an analogy in the comparison of home-baked with factory-baked, sliced, wrapped bread. The quality of the former will vary significantly between households, and its quality will be a matter of local knowledge; the uniform quality of the latter will, in contrast, be generally widely diffused. In much the same way as the standardisation of the factory loaf results in a different product from that of the home producer, so the standardised certification of school and college graduates results in a different type of educational product.

Given then that our attention is to be confined to the activities of educational establishments—schools and colleges—some of the remaining statistical points may be briefly noted. The main problem is that of deciding which establishments are included within the educational sector and which excluded. The treatment of this problem varies both as between countries and within countries over periods of time, so that statistics for different countries and different time-periods may not be fully comparable. Much of the nursery-type of schooling for younger children, for example, is excluded from educational statistics in many countries. Again, commercially-oriented courses such as secretarial preparation in typewriting, shorthand etc. may be excluded, if given by institutions specialising in these spheres, though they may be included if given in schools covering a wider spread of subjects. At the higher levels of education, teaching institutions such as universities will normally be included, while research institutions may be excluded. This can produce anomalies in that students doing post-graduate work will be counted into the educational sector if they are in universities, but excluded if in research organisations. The list could be extended to illustrate how statistical boundaries, however carefully defined, will almost invariably give rise to some elements of artificiality and arbitrariness; the dangers of mechanistic comparisons of such statistics will therefore be apparent.

II

Having thus sounded the warning, the most appropriate way of sketching in the salient features of demand for education is by making some crude assessment of the relative scale of effort in various countries, and the way in which this scale has been evolving over the years.

Perhaps the simplest way to illustrate the absolute state of educational activity is to see what proportion it constitutes of total expenditure or income. For a country as a whole this is done by calculating educational spending as a proportion of national expenditure, the usual measures of which are Gross National Product at market prices, or National Income. Statistics on national income and expenditure now appear on a regular basis for virtually all countries and are reasonably comparable in content and coverage. Educational spending statistics are in a less happy state; though the situation has shown a marked improvement during the present decade. For many countries adequate data is confined to public sector spending, which fortunately in most cases accounts for the bulk of spending. Edding presents data for such spending for twenty-three countries around the year 1960, which shows Finland at 6·6 per cent and the U.S.A. at 6·2 per cent as the countries devoting the largest fraction of the national income to education (the U.S. figures include both public and private spending).[1] Of the remaining twenty-one countries, seven (including Japan, Sweden and Canada) were spending over 5 per cent, three (including the U.K.) more than 4 per cent, five (including West Germany and France) more than 3 per cent, leaving six (including Brazil and India) below the 3 per cent level. Edding also includes a 'guesstimate' for the U.S.S.R. (for which statistics are not available in a comparable form) of 7 per cent.

These data show that education is a major sector of the economy in each of these countries, there being few other

---

[1]'Expenditure on Education' in *Economics of Education*, ed. E. Robinson and J. Vaizey for the International Economic Association, London 1965.

industries or services which claim such a large share of total spending.

While absolute measures of this type serve as a useful point of departure, the more interesting economic questions concern the trends in spending, and the factors which influence it. Edding shows that for each one of his sample countries the percentage of income spent on education rose during the 1950s. In some cases the increase was dramatic, as with Finland where the 1950 figure of 2·6 per cent shot up to 6·6 per cent ten years later; in others it was relatively mild, as with Japan where the increase was from 4·8 per cent to 5·3 per cent. The widespread nature of these increases suggests that the growing importance of education in the post-war period has been intensified. But a more interesting aspect for economists is that such a trend must be unstable because if it continued indefinitely the rising share of income which education absorbed would ultimately approach 100 per cent! It may be taken as axiomatic then that such trends as these cannot be stable over prolonged periods.

One way of establishing this instability would be to examine similar data for a number of separate time periods. Unfortunately this cannot readily be done for most areas, because the compilation of national income data has only really been developed in the past three to four decades. However, for a limited number of countries, the available data provides a useful illustration of past trends. Thus Edding quotes long-term data for the U.S., Germany and Japan which show that downward as well as upward movements have occurred in the educational share of national income. For the U.S. this share was estimated as 2·3 per cent in 1909, 1·6 per cent in 1917, 3·7 per cent in 1927, 5·7 per cent in 1933, 4·1 per cent in 1937, 2·1 per cent in 1943, and 4 per cent in 1949, thereafter rising to the 6·1 per cent recorded for 1959. Similarly, for Germany the 1913 figure was 2·8 per cent, rising to 3·6 per cent in 1927, and to 4·4 per cent in 1933, then falling to 3·1 per cent in 1937. For the post-war years the data relating to West Germany show a steady rise from 3·2 per cent in 1950 to 3·8 per cent in 1960. The Japanese data, which cover the 1930–60 period, show similar fluctuations: the 1930 percentage of 3·9 per cent is followed by a steady fall to the war-time low of 1·95 per cent in

1944; thereafter the post-war rise reaches a peak of 6·1 per cent in 1954 after which there is a regular decline to the 1960 figure of 5·4 per cent.

While, then, the long-term trend during the present century in the relative importance of education appears to have been upwards, this increase has by no means been a regular or continuous one. Many of the shorter-term fluctuations which are indicated by the above data could of course be the result of factors unconnected with education itself. The war years—when a considerable share of the available resources in combatant countries was allocated to military uses, thus lowering the income share of other activities—are a good illustration of this point. The relative share of income devoted to one activity such as education may then change, not because of any absolute movement in the activity itself, but because other components of the national income have altered. Hence care is always needed in the interpretation of a relative measure of this type, if the intention is to derive any conclusions from it.

For our purposes, however, such data suffice to illustrate that education has been growing in relative importance and that it now utilises a significant fraction of available resources in most countries. These statements could be elaborated by recourse to data for the absolute level of educational activity such as numbers of pupils, teachers, schools and so forth, which would illustrate the expansion that has taken place.

At this stage, however, the object is to look at the pattern of demand in order to see which aspects, if any, would warrant more detailed economic analysis. For analytical purposes the factors influencing demand are generally classified into three groups, namely income effects, price effects and the tastes and preferences of customers. The same sequence will be followed here.

III

First let us look at the association between income levels and spending on education. One aspect of this was touched upon only in a general way above, namely that the proportion of income spent on education would rise during a period in which education remained unchanged, but national income fell. One solution to this type of problem, is to calculate the 'income-elasticity of demand', that is, to calculate how demand changes as income changes. If expenditure is taken as being the measurement of demand, this income-elasticity measure can be calculated by comparing the rate of change in educational spending with the rate of change in national income (or expenditure). Rates of change can be established in two ways. One is by analysing the income and spending data at different points in time for the same spending units (countries, individuals etc.), that is by the use of what is termed time-series analysis; the second method is to analyse different spending units at the same point in time, that is, to use what is termed cross-section analysis. Neither method can, of course, give a true measure of the effect which income changes have on the item in question; the time-series because people's habits and tastes may alter over time as do their incomes, the cross-section approach because while it eliminates the time problem, it has to rely on different spending units that may have different basic tastes. In combination, the methods can, however, give a reasonable picture of the likely association between income changes and expenditure changes for the selected activity.

One of the most comprehensive of the available cross-section studies for education is that by Blot and Debeauvais.[2] Using data for more than 100 countries, the relationships between income and spending on education were analysed first for the total population and secondly per head of population. The countries were in turn classified both on a geographical basis and in terms of income per head of population. The results obtained are summarised in the tables overleaf.

The aggregate results indicate an elasticity somewhat in excess of one, meaning that for every 1 per cent rise in income, there was a more than 1 per cent rise in spending on education. Within these aggregate results, however, there are some significant variations in the sub-groups. Perhaps the most striking of

[2]D. Blot and M. Debeauvais, 'Educational Expenditure in Developing Areas'. in *Financing of Education for Economic Growth*, O.E.C.D., Paris 1966.

TABLE 2·1 (a)

Estimated Income Elasticity of Educational Expenditure in 1960: (a) total elasticity (b) per head of population; countries grouped geographically.

Group of Countries	Number	(a) Total Elasticity	(b) Per capita Elasticity
African	35	1·006	1·135
Asian	19	·776	1·333
Latin American	20	1·032	1·303
Industrialised	19	1·101	1·059
All countries	95[3]	1·069	1·241

TABLE 2·1 (b)

Estimated Income Elasticity as above in 1961, countries grouped by income per head

Group of Countries	Number	(a) Total Elasticity	(b) Per capita Elasticity
Less than $100	30	·942	1·571
$100 up to $200	27	1·061	·381
$200 ,, ,, $350	15	·984	1·109
$350 ,, ,, $575	10	·980	3·046
$575 ,, ,, $1,000	7	1·123	4·155
$1,000 over above	15	1·008	0·689
All countries	104	1·074	1·223

Source: Blot and Debeauvais, *op. cit.*, 75–8.

[3] The total 95 includes two countries, Spain and Portugal, not included in any of the groups.

these is the very low per capita elasticity of ·381 for the twenty-seven country group in Table 2·1 (b), whose per capita income was between $100 and $200, even though the aggregate elasticity of 1·061 was about average. This might be taken to suggest that these countries, while expanding their aggregate spending at a rate similar to that of the other groups, were finding it difficult to keep abreast of population expansion. Blot and Debeauvais, however, warn against the drawing of any specific conclusions of this sort, because of possible imperfections in the data, allied to the general difficulty of deriving valid international comparisons from aggregate calculations of this type. Moreover, in the specific example quoted, the calculated value of ·381 was one of the few which did not meet the statistical significance tests applied to all of their calculations. In part, this could be the result of the purely arbitrary groupings which were used; a point which the authors discuss. The results of calculations using a different grouping (less than $150, $150–$300, $300–$600 etc.) show for the nearest comparable group—the twenty-five countries in the range $150 to $300—a per capita elasticity of ·680. Again however, this fails to meet the tests of statistical significance. The results for other groupings which are given further reinforce the authors' point, that the grouping selected has a substantial influence on the results obtained. Their general conclusion on this aspect of their study is that while information of this type can be of great value it seems rather doubtful whether operational conclusions should be drawn on the basis of these statistical results.

For these latter purposes Blot and Debeauvais suggest that time-series data for countries would be more appropriate. Though they do not present such data they refer to some calculations of this nature which they prepared for several industrialised countries during the post-war period. In each case the elasticities obtained were considerably greater than one. Their time-series analysis thus apparently yielded elasticities of higher values than those recorded by their cross-section study. This is a result of some interest because the usual expectation in analyses of expenditure patterns is that the result would be the other way around, with the cross-section study yielding the higher results. This is because cross-section studies will be affected by various short-term fluctuations and variations between the spending units sampled, whereas time-series analysis over a sustained period will give an opportunity for such influences to cancel out.

While there do not appear to be any time-series studies of a comparable nature available to explore this aspect more fully, some approximate calculations can be carried out for the data which are available. A convenient illustration is provided by U.K. data compiled by Vaizey, which is a useful example because it provides estimates of both public and private expenditure on education for the years 1920, 1925, 1930, 1935, 1940, 1945, 1950 and 1955.[4] By relating the changes in spending recorded at those dates with changes in national income over the same periods, the following estimated elasticities were obtained:

TABLE 2·2

Estimated Income Elasticities (unadjusted) of Current Educational Spending. U.K. selected time-periods for (a) public spending (b) private spending

Period	Estimated Elasticity (a)	Elasticity (b)
1920–25	−1·0	−0·4
1925–30	2·1	−2·0
1930–35	0·2	−0·2
1935–40	0·3	0·4
1940–45	0·6	2·2
1945–50	3·8	0·9
1950–55	1·2	0·3
1920–55	2·4	1·4

Source: based on data in Vaizey, *op. cit.*, 78, table III.

The first observation to make on these estimates is that they are not elasticity measures in the correct sense because they are

[4] *The Costs of Education*, London 1958.

based on data given in current prices, so that some of the
changes could have been due to price movements. The reasons
for not presenting any correction for price movements will
emerge later when the problems of obtaining constant price
data are touched upon. Apart from this problem, the estimates
show a wide range of results. For the different five-year periods
no systematic pattern appears to be present, with high elasticities in some periods succeeded by low ones in others. The
interpretation of the negative figures is that the national
income and educational spending series moved in opposite
directions to each other during these periods. Thus in the
1920–25 period the national income (in current prices) fell,
but educational spending, both public and private, rose;
between 1925–30 income rose but private spending fell,
while between 1930–35 income fell and private spending
rose.

In addition to the effect which changing price levels would
have on these results, other external factors could influence the
data. One such factor, mentioned by Vaizey, is the variations
in the number of births which naturally affected the size of the
school-going population. Thus there were substantial falls in
births in the mid-1920s and in the war years, with rapid
increases in the late 1920s and again in the 1950s. Such
changes would probably affect spending on the compulsory
educational age groups since provision would be needed for all
children in this category. Calculations per head of population
would help to correct this factor to some extent, though not
completely, since such data would only adjust for changes in the
total number of inhabitants in the country, but not for changes
in their age-composition.

One point of interest for our purposes at this stage, however,
is that for the period as a whole the estimated elasticities are
considerably in excess of one and this is the case with both
public and private spending, so that the results are consistent
with those of Blot and Debeauvais. A second feature is that the
elasticity for private spending is lower than that for public
spending, meaning that the latter has grown at the faster rate.
This is the trend which has characterised the majority of
countries in recent years, though the data for the U.S. presented

by Machlup show that private spending had grown more rapidly in the U.S. over the period 1920–60.[5]

Some further appreciation of the manner in which income changes may affect spending may be possible in the case of private expenditure, by the use of more detailed data for different income and family groups. Such data are generally obtained by collecting information on income/expenditure for samples of households. The subsequent analysis of the data may permit the formulation and testing of hypotheses concerning consumer behaviour. One hypothesis which may be relevant to educational spending is the concept of a 'threshold' income above which there is a disproportionate rise in the amount of 'discretionary' income at the consumer's disposal. The reasoning is that at low income levels the bulk, if not the whole, of available income is, in effect, automatically earmarked for obtaining necessities. As income rises there is a wider range of choice or discretion in the consumer's spending, which among other things will mean that items can now be purchased which hitherto could not be afforded, or else were severely rationed. The extra discretionary spending will primarily affect what are conventionally described as luxury goods. The analysis could also apply to education, however, especially in countries where there is a mixed system of free or low-cost publicly-financed schools and higher-cost private schools. In such situations consumers may decide to spend part of their higher incomes on the more costly forms of education.

One illustration of the more detailed data is the Irish household budget survey of 1951–52 which subsequently has been analysed in some detail by Leser.[6] Expenditure patterns were analysed by size of family, social group and income level. As one would expect, size of family influenced household expenditure on education. Thus for households with the same income level, those with two adults but no children were spending 2·1 per cent of income on education, compared with 4·1 per cent for those with two adults and two children, and 5·3 per cent for households of two adults and four children. The

[5] *The Production and Distribution of Knowledge in the United States*, Princeton 1962.
[6] *A Further Analysis of Irish Household Budget Data*, Paper No. 23, Economic Research Institute, Dublin 1964.

analysis of spending by social group showed that for each of the four income groups used, the proportion of income spent on education was higher for middle-class than for working-class families; a result which is consistent with data obtained in other countries. The more interesting result, however, lay in the rate of change of such spending; for the middle-class groups the data yielded an income-elasticity of 1·9, whereas for the working-class groups the figure was 3·5.

The interpretation of these figures is that while the absolute fraction of income spent on education was lower for the working-class groups, their spending was rising at a faster rate as income increased. In terms of the 'threshold' hypothesis these results would suggest either that the 'threshold' is located at different income levels for the two social groups, or that the rates of increase beyond the threshold are different in each case. But again, of course, the usual cautions must attach to any attempted interpretation; in this particular instance the main reservations are that the results could have been affected by sampling errors, by inaccurate replies to the questionnaires, or by local variations in the price and availability of education which would influence the spending needed to buy any given amount of education.

The relevance of these more detailed analyses of spending is that they can aid in building up an understanding of the way in which the aggregate pattern of educational spending may alter as national income changes. The household budget data suggest, for example, that if there are shifts in the distribution of income over time, between groups with different spending patterns, whether they be different social groups, households of different size, or whatever, such shifts will lead to different expenditure in the aggregate.

Finally, before leaving this question of the association between income and spending on education, one further point may be noted, namely that any causal link between the two could originate from either item, that is, spending on education might change because income had changed, but also income might alter because spending on education had moved. The question of the possible causal links between the two series is a problem which will arise in the later chapters.

IV

The second influence on demand to be discussed, namely the behaviour of prices, is an aspect of considerable difficulty in the case of education. A major reason for this is the absence of a 'price' for much educational activity, since it is provided free of direct charge by governments or other agencies. This is a problem not unique to education, since it arises with any goods or services provided 'free'. A second reason, and one which is again not unique to education, but which applies in particular to many service activities, is that there is no direct measure of the 'output' which is sold. As a result of these complications there is a certain degree of ambiguity attached to the concept of prices in education. The normal object in separating price movements from other influences on demand is, in the terminology of economics, to permit movements along given demand schedules to be distinguished from shifts between different demand schedules. The problem can be illustrated by using the customary price-quantity diagram, as in Figure 1. The demand

FIGURE I

Hypothetical Demand Schedules for X

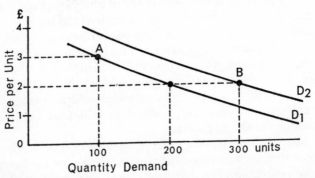

Quantity Demand

schedule, which illustrates the relationship between price and quantity required, is depicted as sloping downwards to the right, indicating that the lower the price the greater the quantity which will be demanded. This is the relationship postulated for the majority of items, though there are some exceptions to it. A price-quantity demand schedule also requires some other assumptions. One is the *ceteris paribus* assumption (that all other aspects are taken as given), a second is that the item X can be adequately distinguished. The diagram illustrates the separate influences which price and income may have on demand. Schedule D1 shows that at a price of £3 per unit, 100 units will be demanded whereas if the price were reduced to £2, 200 units would be required. The effect of an income change can be shown by inserting a second schedule, D2, which lies to the right of D1. This is taken as representing a higher level of income than that on which D1 was based, since at all prices a greater quantity is demanded than is the case with D1. At a price of £3, for example, 200 units are desired, while at £2 the quantity rises to 300. Once the size of the income change associated with the shift from D1 to D2 is specified, the income-elasticity measure discussed above can be calculated. It will be apparent, however, that the resulting figure will differ for each different price level. Suppose, for example, that the income increase was 25 per cent. At a price of £3 the resulting increase in demand is from 100 to 200 units or a rise of 100 per cent, and the measured income-elasticity would then be 4 (100 per cent ÷ 25 per cent). At a price of £2, however, the rise in demand is from 200 to 300 units; an increase of 50 per cent, which results in a measured elasticity of 2. To derive a true income-elasticity measurement it is therefore necessary to specify, *inter alia*, the necessary price levels. This was not, of course, done in the crude calculations given earlier.

Similar remarks would apply to any measurements of price-elasticity of demand, that is, the change in quantity demanded that is associated with a price change. For schedule D1 a price fall of 33⅓ per cent (from £3 to £2) is associated with a quantity change of 100 per cent (from 100 to 200), yielding a price-elasticity which will be taken as 3 (100 per cent ÷ 33⅓ per cent).[7]

[7]This is not mathematically accurate since the formula used here (proportionate changes in the quantity demanded divided by the proportionate price change) is only valid for marginal, that is, infinitesimally small, changes, and is the elasticity at one *point* on the schedule. For such large finite changes as those used here, an arc-elasticity measure is needed. Such refinements need not, however, delay us here. The interested reader may be referred to any comprehensive textbook treatment of demand theory, e.g. G. Stigler, *Theory of Price*, New York 1952, 35.

B

For schedule D2 on the other hand, the same fall in price is associated with a 50 per cent quantity change, yielding an elasticity of 1·5.

The normal situation in practice is that both price and income changes occur side by side, so that in one year a position such as that marked A may be observed, while in a later year, the position has changed to B. The task is then to disentangle price movements from income changes which go to make up the movement from A to B. In order to do this, one prerequisite is the ability to establish the price of X at both dates. In the case of education, both of the difficulties indicated above will be encountered here, namely, that much education is provided free, and that there is no clearly measurable product to which any price might correspond. It might appear that the latter statement is not correct since fees are charged by various institutions which are identifiable as regards both the level and the quality of their courses. Harvard, for example, is and has been identifiable as providing university education, in contrast to schools such as Eton which cater for pre-university studies. Quality is a more nebulous concept, but there is a sense in which the various establishments will be ranked, however crudely, on this basis. It would thus seem that the price for education of a specified type could be distinguished in the same way as the prices of, say, sports cars or limousines. What is normally absent from the educational measure however is any adjustment for quality changes over time. For most subjects a university degree today will not, for example, describe the same product as the same qualifications fifty years ago, given the changes in knowledge which have taken place during that time, but such improvements would need to be taken into account when comparing prices at both dates as otherwise the cost of producing a course of the same quality at the later date would be overstated.

The same sort of problem arises with all products and requires careful data recording in order to disentagle price changes due to quality improvements from cost-induced price rises. In principle the same efforts could be made for education but existing data do not permit any adequate treatment of the problem. Two of the more obvious obstacles with the existing position are first that the 'product' is not as unambiguously defined with education (e.g. is it only the graduate who is a product of a university, or should those who drop-out at various stages be included?) and secondly, that the prices charged do not relate to the costs of providing the various subjects.

This non-business approach is reflected in the treatment actually accorded to education in national income statistics, where the volume and price of educational activity is calculated from the input, and not the output, side, that is, the payments for teachers, equipment, materials etc., are used as measures. This is comparable to measuring industrial 'output' in terms of the 'input' of labour, raw materials etc., instead of the products which it has manufactured or sold. The need to rely on this 'input' type of measurement for education arises not only from the difficulties which exist with that segment of education sold on a fee basis, but also from the presence of 'free' education. Clearly with this latter form of education no direct price can be obtained on an output basis since there is no financial transaction taking place between the consumer and the educational supplier.

Movements in the price of education, as measured by price movements in the various inputs, will clearly exclude any improvements in the quality of the output provided or any other form of productivity rise, hence there is a built-in bias with this type of measurement towards a long-term rise in the price of education relative to other prices. Teachers' salaries, for example, to take one major input, may be expected to increase over time, both as compensation for any general rise in the cost of living, and also as a consequence of overall increases in productivity per head.

Increases of the latter type raise the real income of teachers and are the mechanism by which they share in the increased output and living standards of the economy. But given that input is also the measure of output for education, any such rise in teachers' salaries will raise the price of education. The importance of this price factor as a contributor to changes in total cost can be illustrated by the following data taken from an American study:

TABLE 2·3

Increases in Costs of U.S. Public Schools 1929/30 *to* 1955/56

Factor Causing Increase	Per Cent of Total Increase
Enrolment increase	6·2
Reduction of pupil/teacher ratio	5·3
Operating and maintenance costs	7·6
Administration costs	3·6
Additional auxiliary services	10·2
Additional instruction services	4·0
Fixed charges	6·3
Rise in teachers' *real* salaries	36·2
Price inflation	20·6
	100·0

Of the total rise in costs (or expenditure), the 6 per cent increase in pupils was the only quantity increase. The reduction in the pupil/teacher ratio, meaning smaller classes, and the additional services which were provided may be taken as quality improvements. Twenty per cent of the increases were the consequence of general price rises in the economy, which led both to higher prices of purchased materials etc. and to increases in teachers' salaries to maintain their living standards. The largest component in the overall increase was, however, the further rise in teachers' pay which raised their real incomes, and this indicates the strength of the tendency towards built-in relative price increases in cases where reliance must be placed on an input measure of price.

A further complication in attempting to discuss price changes over time in the case of education is that any shifts which have taken place in the proportion of cost met by the consumer and that borne from other sources will affect the position. An illustration of such a shift is provided by the post-war situation in the U.K. with regard to university fees. As a result of the system of student grants introduced in this period, the bulk of the fees charged are paid from these grants and not by the student (or his parents). Hence, so far as the student is concerned, university education is now 'cheaper' than in pre-war days, when the fees were largely met from the student's own resources. While such changes in financing methods do not by themselves alter the price to the community as a whole, they do re-allocate this total as between recipients and non-recipients of the educational service in question. The price which would enter into any aggregate calculation for the entire economy would consequently be different from that relating to any studies dealing with individuals or groups.

The ambiguity in the concept of price is more general than this since there are numerous other changes which would affect the price of education to various groups, and many of these changes would not be reflected by any measure of educational activity as such. The introduction of a new school into an area may, for example, result in a reduction in transport costs for pupils; this would constitute an effective lowering in the price of education so far as they were concerned, but would statistically appear as a fall in consumer spending on transport services. The total cost or price of education is not simply the expenses associated with educational institutions, but embraces all costs which must be incurred in order to participate in the specified educational activity. This is a subject which will be taken up again in the next chapter. Enough has been written at this juncture to illustrate why the customary economic analysis of price relationships cannot readily be applied in the sphere of education.

V

The third influence on spending listed above was that of tastes and preferences. As used in economic discussion this is a residual category in that any change in demand which cannot be attributed to a price or income change is deemed to be a result of change in people's tastes. The explanation of any such shifts is not something which economists undertake; they leave these problems to psychologists, sociologists and other behavioural scientists. The economist will, however, be interested in whatever data can be provided on the characteristics affecting spending, since they will aid in building up an understanding of the demand pattern. In the educational case, data on both individual and governmental characteristics would be useful, given that both sectors account for significant expenditures.

In the case of individuals, the household budget type of survey illustrated earlier is one useful source of data since it provides information on the household characteristics associated with various expenditure patterns. Middle-class and working-class families in the same income group were, for example, seen to have different educational expenditures in the illustration quoted. Assuming that similar schools were available to each group (so that the 'price' of education was comparable for each) these indicate different preferences for education on the part of each group. More extensive surveys can provide data on more of the characteristics associated with differential spending.

One of the more comprehensive of such studies in the educational sphere is that made for a sample of about 3,000 U.S. households by Morgan and others.[8] As one part of this study, the characteristics of the household heads associated with differences in the amount of education (measured by number of years' study) received by their children were analysed. In all, thirteen characteristics were examined, namely, the education of the household head, education of wife, education level of heads' fathers, occupation, age, race, religion, number of children, age of head at birth of eldest child, peak earnings, need-achievement and work attitude, rural-urban migration, and south-north migration. Ten of these variables yielded results which were statistically significant, meaning that they

[8]J. Morgan, M. David, W. Cohen, H. Brazer, *Income and Welfare in the U.S.*, McGraw-Hill 1962.

were unlikely to be the result of random chance. The factors
having the largest effect on the education of the children were
the education of the household head and of his wife, his
occupation and the number of children. This study suggests
that the pattern of educational demand is the result of a
complex set of forces; more complex even than the results
suggest, for, as the authors point out, there are several respects
in which the study was not as helpful as they would have
wished. In the first instance the variables studied 'explained' (in
statistical terms) only 41 per cent of the observed variations in
the educational experience of the children studied. One reason
given for this was the inability to take any account of differences
in the abilities of the children themselves; a factor which could
clearly affect their education. A second reason was that the
treatment of the relationship between household income and
education of children was unsatisfactory. The income measure
used—peak earnings—was adopted because it was thought that
it would be the best indicator for cases where people had retired
from work, or for those whose incomes had declined since the
periods when their children had been at schools. The data
actually obtained for this measure may have been affected by
memory errors, by abnormal earnings for a brief period or by
price inflation which would cause the same reported income
figure to relate to different real income positions depending on
the year(s) in which the peak income was earned. The data on
peak earnings are, then, not necessarily an accurate reflection
of lifetime earnings nor of ability to finance children's education. The authors in fact suggest that both the education and
occupation of the household heads may be more closely
associated with real relative lifetime earnings than their figure
for peak earnings.

One of the more technical problems with studies of this type
is that the various factors, all of which are treated separately
for statistical purposes, may well be interdependent to some
extent. The authors suggest, for example, that occupations,
peak earnings, age at birth of first child and number of children,
probably derive some of their impact on education of children
because of their relationship to lifetime earnings and hence to
the capacity to pay for higher education. For statistical analysis

of this type the assumption is that each of the factors studied affects the item in question in a manner which is independent of the values shown by the other explanatory factors. It presumes, for example, that variations in the education of the household head always affect the education of the children to the same extent, regardless of the values for other characteristics such as age, race or occupation. As the authors recognise, such an assumption is not fully realistic, and would produce absurd results in some instances. To cope to some extent with this problem, analyses were made for some sub-groups within the total sample; for example the pattern associated with white, male, non-farm spending units was separately analysed from that of the total sample.

A further interesting feature of this study was the fact that in addition to the analysis of the relationships between household heads and the education of their children, an examination was also made of the relationships between these heads and their parents. This part of the study suggests that the characteristics affecting education remain relatively stable over long periods of time. Eleven factors were used in this part of the study, eight of which were similar to those used in the earlier part. The most important of the variables chosen was again parental education; in this case the education of their fathers being the most significant factor associated with the educational level of the household heads. Of the other factors studied, the most important in this section were the ages of the household heads themselves and their fathers' occupations.

This study is valuable in that it demonstrates educational demand as being systematically linked with various socio-economic characteristics of households, and that these relationships appear to hold relatively stable over time. A second example of the intergenerational influence on educational demand is furnished for the U.K. by the Robbins report.[9] The following table summarises the relevant data for a sample of students.

[9]*Higher Education*, Report of the Committee on Higher Education, H.M.S.O., London 1963.

TABLE 2·4

Highest level of education for a sample of children born in 1940/41, classified by parental education (%)

Parental Education	Education of Child			
	Full-time higher education		No full-time higher education	Total
	(a) degree	(b) other	education	Total
Age on completing full-time education				
[A] Father—18 or over	32	11	57	100
16–17	14	7	79	100
Under 16	2	3	95	100
[B] Mother—18 or over	25	10	65	100
16–17	19	8	73	100
Under 16	2	3	95	100

Source: Report on Higher Education, *op. cit.,* Appendix One, p. 60.

The strong association between a high level of parental education and a high level of education for the child is evident from this table, and is reinforced by further data in the same appendix which show for the same sample of children that only 3 per cent of those whose fathers completed education at 18 plus finished school before 16, compared with 32 per cent for those whose fathers finished at 16–17, and 76 per cent for those whose fathers finished school before 16.

Various other factors associated with educational experience were also investigated in the Robbins report, some of which, such as parental occupation, social class and size of family were similar to those analysed in the U.S. study. Again, in the British case each of these factors was associated with significant variations in the educational experience of children. The Robbins study also presents data on some of the internal educational characteristics, such as the size of class in the primary and secondary schools, and the percentage of the children who attended grammar type secondary schools, which suggest that school environment aspects also influence educational experience.

The list of examples citing characteristics associated with the amount of education acquired by various categories of children could be extended, but those quoted are sufficient to illustrate the point that the pattern of demand for education by individuals is systematically influenced by a wide range of socioeconomic factors. Such information is valuable since it helps both in estimating the probable course of future demand and also, if the pattern is deemed unsatisfactory, in indicating possible areas for changes in educational policy by government or other interested agencies.

It should be explained however that while data of the foregoing type are useful, they are not by themselves adequate for identifying the actual motivations for education, or the relative importance of any one influence, both of which would be necessary before any useful conclusions could be drawn. The observed falling off in the proportion of children from lower social groups going on to higher levels of education, for example, lends itself to a mixture of both economic and non-economic interpretations. A sociological interpretation would be to attribute differences in the desire for education to the influence of social class. This form of interpretation would suggest for example that the traditional working-class culture is an active hindrance to taking up educational opportunity even if it is provided. In part this is because group solidarity is valued more than the individual achievement and success which may carry a price in the form of separation from less successful relatives and friends. It is also held to be partly due to working-class groups being less habituated than middle classes to making long-term life plans, both because working-class plans may be more frequently disrupted by unemployment and other factors, and because they are less accustomed to making the savings which are needed to finance any long-term plans. In addition to general differences of this kind in the preferences of the various social groups, it has also been suggested that a bias of a more specifically educational nature could also exist. This more specific bias would arise if, as is held, schools reflect and transmit predominantly middle-class rather than working-class values and culture. If this were the case, it would have the effect of lowering the amount of satisfaction which working-class students obtained by comparison with their middle-class counterparts.

It is equally possible to postulate more economically-based interpretations. If education were sought, not as an end in itself, but because it is useful for, say, raising earning power in later life, then differences in demand for education as between social groups could be the result of differences in the returns which they expected to earn on this education. Such differences could arise in at least two ways. First, children of working-class origin might on average be less able than their middle-class counterparts, or even where they have the same initial ability, their attainment at school may on average be lower (possibly for the cultural reasons given above). Secondly, even where educational attainments are similar, the subsequent earnings of those from working-class origins may prove to be lower. Both of these factors would have the effect of making education a less attractive economic proposition to working-class families; the first by lowering the expectation of success for any pupil, the second by reducing the absolute size of the return to be gained from investing in education.

A somewhat different explanation would be to attribute much of the observed variation between the groups to differences in the degree of information which they possessed concerning education. The more educated parents are more likely to be better 'informed' of the value of education, whether as an item in its own right or as worthwhile investment. If this were so, the lower participation by working-class groups could occur even though their basic preferences might be similar to those of the middle-class, and the economic returns equal, because of their ignorance of the situation. On a more general plane, this argument of lack of information can be used as a reason why economists might support campaigns for extending adequate education to all citizens, because it is necessary for consumers to possess an adequate degree of information before a competitive market economy can function efficiently. Education, especially of the formal school type envisaged here, need not necessarily be the most efficient method of providing this information since education and information are not identical. Moreover, the relevant information is that concerning prices and other phenomena governing the various markets in which the individual buys and sells. Education, however, is seen as one of the best devices by which individuals acquire the necessary techniques for the acquisition and analysis of information on any specific area; in other words it may be a kind of necessary infrastructure on which these subsequent informational activities can be based. The relevance of this apparent digression to the interpretation of educational participation is that differences in information concerning education may be classified as an economic or non-economic aspect according to one's viewpoint.

Having thus illustrated some of the possible inferences which could be drawn from the data on the characteristics associated with variations in educational levels, it might well be asked whether a simpler approach to the problem of interpretation would be to ask the students themselves their reasons for seeking education. Such an approach would scarcely be relevant for education in the compulsory age-groups, but it has been applied to the later years of education in several instances. The results of one such study have been summarised by Harris as follows:

> In a survey undertaken by the Educational Testing Service for the Natural Science Foundation, among the 11,000 boys who replied, more than 4,000 went to college because they needed a degree to work, 2,300 because they wanted to increase their earning power, and 1,400 to explore the kinds of work they wanted to do. Only 392 went to college because they enjoyed studying; 505 sought social development and 287 responded to social pressures. Among the girls the structure of replies was not greatly different though they emphasised much more a desire for

social development. Roughly 7,500 out of the 12,000 who replied stated that they were primarily interested in the vocational aspects.[10]

The results of such survey are open to the usual reservations: they may contain sampling errors, the answers may be affected by the form in which the questions are asked, or by respondents wishing to give answers which they think are expected of them. This American study is nevertheless of interest to the economist since it suggests that economic considerations are one of the dominant factors for those who participate in higher education.

VI

The remaining task is to consider briefly the characteristics of public sector demand for education. Clearly, methods used in examining the tastes and preferences of individuals cannot be applied to this area of demand; the discussion must therefore be confined to a more general exposition of the apparent objectives of public sector activities in education. Such objectives are rarely defined with great precision; nevertheless it seems possible to identify the more important factors which have been operative and to observe the way in which objectives undergo subtle transformations in the light of new knowledge or influences.

In the earlier stages of public intervention in education the prime emphasis is generally on ensuring that all children (or at least the vast majority) will receive some minimum amount of education. The actual measures used to achieve this objective will vary with the existing circumstances of the economy, but the most frequently observed pattern is one of introducing legislation to make education compulsory for children of certain ages, ensuring that schools are made available either by introducing a governmentally-operated network or by providing funds for privately-managed schools, and making education 'free' in the sense that pupils are not charged fees for

[10]S. Harris, *Economic Aspects of Higher Education*, O.E.C.D., Paris 1964.

attending. All of these measures need not necessarily be used simultaneously. In the U.K., for example, the 1870 Act empowered local educational boards to provide school facilities for all children of school age (5–13 years), but elementary education did not become compulsory until 1880, and fees were only finally abolished in 1918, though they had ceased to be important following the fee-grants in 1891. At the present time, however, the vast majority of underdeveloped countries—which are today the areas where this first stage of public sector provision is still an important one—have taken all three steps.

In this first stage the emphasis of public sector activity is likely to be on quantity rather than quality; wider questions such as the attainment levels of pupils or the extent to which different groups of children respond to the available facilities tend to be relegated to a subsidiary role. As one author, writing of the U.K., expresses it: 'The basic aim of our first great education statute, the Elementary Education Act of 1870, was to get the children to school, and there was a strong tendency to assume that securing attendance at school was equivalent to education.'[11] As this first global objective was attained, the emphasis in state activity shifted towards more localised or more qualitative aims. At the level of compulsory education, for example, school meals and school health services were introduced, in part perhaps as a component of social services generally, but partly because of the recognition that under-nourished or sick children would not derive maximum educational benefit from school attendance. These types of ancillary services may then be regarded as an attempt to cater for the educational needs of specific sectors of the school-going population.

Beyond the level of compulsory education, efforts were also directed towards removing the obstacles which might prevent some children from staying on at school. The more obvious example of these activities was the rise in scholarship schemes designed to remove the financial obstacles confronting many children. This attempt to remove, or at least reduce, any external barriers to educational participation, may be taken as

[11]W. O. Lester Smith, *Education*, London 1962, 13.

marking the introduction of a new policy objective: the social objective of producing equality of opportunity. In its earlier forms the concept of equal opportunity was regarded as an attempt to ensure that access to the available educational facilities would be on the basis of the pupils' merit or ability, and not the result of external factors such as parental income, race, sex, or religion. The U.K., for example, provided an extensive system of grants, the sizes of which were related to family income and circumstances, for pupils at both the secondary and higher levels of education. Examination or selection procedures were introduced in order to determine which children should be eligible for these awards.

While many hoped that schemes of this U.K. type would provide a satisfactory degree of educational opportunity for all children, the post-war decades have witnessed a growing disenchantment with this view. The awareness of the complexities involved in such objectives has been heightened as a consequence of an international flow of sociological, psychological and educational research showing that disparities in educational participation are associated with the subtle interaction of many social/economic factors. This has produced a shift in policy emphasis in at least two areas. First there is the recognition that the pattern of school organisation, the type of curricula available and other characteristics internal to the educational system itself affect the performance of different groups in varying ways. Secondly, there has been acceptance of the view that observed ability is not wholly the result of the innate characteristics of children but is partly influenced by the environment to which they are exposed, especially in their early years. These two aspects have led to the concept of educational opportunity being reformulated in terms of providing positive educational discrimination in favour of those children who suffer from these environmental handicaps. Some of the implications which these more extensive concepts of educational opportunity may hold for the school system will be examined later (in chapter seven); at this stage it will suffice to note that a social objective of this nature now appears to be a major element of policy in developed countries.

A third type of policy objective which has received emphasis in the past decade has been the economic one of ensuring that the educational system provides the skilled manpower needed in a modern economy. The high rate of scientific and technological innovation, coupled with the post-war acceptance by governments of responsibility for promoting policies of full employment and rising living standards, has resulted in increasing attention to the problems of training adequate numbers of scientific and technical personnel. Apart from normal industrial requirements, the development of complex weapons systems meant that the defence sectors in several countries, notably the U.S.A., experienced a spectacular growth in their demands for highly-qualified personnel. One indicator of this concern with manpower aspects has been the developing programme of educational planning activities by agencies such as UNESCO and O.E.C.D. which have resulted in manpower/education studies and plans being prepared in many member countries.

This brief sketch of the changing nature of governmental interest in education may help to explain at least part of the growth of public spending on education. The movement away from a position where the prime official concern is with the provision of some minimum level of school facilities towards situations in which they become concerned with which groups avail of school, with their level of attainment, with the types of subjects they study, or with the vocational preparation they receive, are all changes likely to call for increased official spending.

VII

The discussion of demand for education has necessarily been of a general and rather inconclusive nature. At this stage the intention has been to show that the conventional approach used for analysing demand for commodities in a market system cannot readily be applied to education, because much of the educative service provided is not channelled through a market system. For this reason no attempt was made to derive any precise measure of prices or income effects on demand, nor to distinguish these from the influences which tastes and preferences, whether of individuals or governments, might have on educational demand.

It is hoped, however, that the discussion is not entirely without value. One positive intention has been to emphasise that demand, as used in an economic sense, can have different connotations from its everyday usage. In economics, any specification of demand always implies that certain price, income and other characteristics must also be specified, to avoid misleading inferences or analyses being made. It has become commonplace, for example, in recent years to refer to a growing 'social demand' for education—the usual connotations being that there has been a growing wish to have more education—or in the terms of the analysis given above, a shift in tastes and preferences. It should now be clear, however, that people may be buying more education (and other items) simply because they have greater incomes today, or because the 'price' of education has been reduced in many cases by government actions. Terms such as social demand may also have both quantitative and qualitative dimensions. As used by some writers, the term refers to the demand for places by parents and pupils,[12] whereas others identify both a 'private' and a 'social' element—the latter given effect by governments—which may harmonise or conflict with each other.[13] These differences and distinctions need not, however, be pursued here.

A second intention has been to demonstrate that there is a variety of motivation for education which may be operative at both the private and public levels, and there is prima facie evidence that among these, economic factors are of some importance. It is proposed in the three ensuing chapters to elaborate more fully the ways in which these economic constituents of educational demand can be dealt with in theoretical and empirical terms.

---

[12]See, e.g., *Educational Policy and Planning: Austria*, O.E.C.D., Paris 1968, 167; or M. Blaug, 'Approaches to Educational Planning', *Economic Journal*, June 1967.
[13]See, e.g., *The Mediterranean Regional Project: Country Reports—Turkey*, O.E.C.D., Paris 1965, 57ff.

CHAPTER 3

EDUCATION AS A PERSONAL INVESTMENT

In this chapter the notion that demand for education by individuals may be economically motivated will be explored. This concept implies that education is bought by people, not for any direct pleasure or satisfaction which it yields to them, but because it raises income or lowers costs, thus indirectly raising the consumption standards of those concerned. In economic terminology, education would then be an investment rather than a consumption item; or in more philosophical language it would be a means to an end, and not an end in itself.

If education is to be viewed in this way, the individual must be able to calculate the profitability of education in order to decide how much he should buy. His approach is effectively the same as that of a businessman deciding, for example, whether to buy more machines for his factory and, if so, how many. In making choices of this nature it is first necessary to have information on the costs and returns of the proposed investment, and then to compare these with the alternative uses to which the same resources of time and money might be put. In other words it is not enough to estimate the profit from the proposed investment; one must decide whether this profit is greater or less than some alternative investment. This latter type of comparison is necessary because the true economic value of a project can only be ascertained when its 'opportunity cost' is known. This opportunity cost, the items which must be forgone when a project is selected, constitutes the real economic measure of cost for all activities.

For calculation of business investments, opportunity cost

calculations are normally made by applying a rate of interest or of discount to all future cost or revenue items. A potential investment project, for example, may call for the expenditure of £100 now and in return it is expected to yield £105 one year from now, the rate of return on cost being then 5 per cent per annum. The expected returns exceed the costs, but before deciding that the project is worthwhile, the opportunity cost calculation will be made by comparing this return with some appropriate interest rate. If this interest rate is, say, 3 per cent the project will be worthwhile since the expected return of 5 per cent is greater than this. Similarly, if the relevant interest rate were 10 per cent the project would be rejected because of its inadequate rate of return. The actual rate of interest (or, possibly more correctly, rates) which a business will apply for these calculations, is that which they can earn on funds by lending them, or which they must pay for borrowed funds. This market rate of interest, the price at which money may be borrowed or lent, measures the opportunity cost of a project because it reflects both the alternative investment and the alternative consumption uses of the required resources. It reflects alternative investment uses because the demand for funds will be based on the estimated profitability of all potential investment opportunities. Equally, it reflects alternative consumption uses because the supply of funds will be based on comparisons by lenders between the utility to them of spending now or of saving (which will permit higher future spending). Demand for funds is, then, a function of what is termed the productivity of investment, while supply is a function of what is termed time-preference between present and future goods. The conventional method of illustrating this process of interest determination is that given in Figure 3.1. The demand schedule is depicted as sloping downwards to the right, implying that not all investment opportunities are equally profitable, so that if they are ranked in order of profitability, the returns from additional investment are gradually diminishing. The supply schedule also follows the conventional pattern of sloping upwards from left to right; the interpretation being that people will not require much compensation by way of interest payments to forgo small amounts of present consumption, but as

FIGURE 3·1

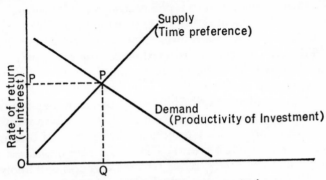

the amounts of funds required rise, so also will the interest rate necessary to compensate them.

It is useful to provide this brief summary of investment appraisal because it will help in the subsequent discussion of both the present and succeeding chapters.

This same process of appraisal is then, in principle, what the economically motivated individual should apply when deciding whether education is a worthwhile purchase. Its application will, therefore, call for the same type of information on costs and returns, together with the identification of a suitable interest rate for opportunity cost comparisons. With activities such as education, however, where the distinction between economic and non-economic components can frequently be rather blurred, it will be useful to explore more fully the distinctions involved in identifying the 'investment' aspects of educational activity.

The usual theoretical distinction between 'consumption' and 'investment' is based on the purpose for which an item is used. The bottle of ink used by one person for writing letters to friends is a 'consumption' item, that used by another for writing books or newspaper articles for payment is an 'investment'. The trouble with this theoretical distinction, however, is that it is virtually impossible to apply in practice, since it is difficult to envisage the collection of data regarding the purpose to which every commodity is put by its purchaser.

In practice the distinction between consumption and investment is drawn by the use of a number of statistical conventions. One is that the classification is made on the basis of final sale rather than of final use. A second distinguishes producing units (firms) from consuming units (households); problems can arise here: self-employed people and government are two examples of categories which may appear as both producers and consumers. A third convention relates to time; measurements of many economic aggregates such as output, consumption and investment use the year as the normal time-span. There are thus four categories to be defined: purchases by firms of items which are used in the same year, purchases by firms of durable items, and purchases by households in the same durable and non-durable categories. In this framework 'investment' refers (with one exception noted below) to durable items bought by firms. A purchase of machinery, for example, is treated as investment because this equipment will (usually!) contribute to output not only in the year of purchase but in succeeding years also. Purchases of raw materials, on the other hand, used for production in the same year, which constitute a type of short-term investment by a firm—since they are a means to an end—are not so described but are placed in a third category termed 'inputs'. In the case of households, non-durable items, food, drink, entertainment etc. are classified as 'consumption'. Durable items such as clothing, washing-machines, motor-cars or houses, which yield a stream of consumption benefits over longish time-periods are more difficult to treat. The arbitrary statistical solution adopted in most countries is to treat all such items with the sole exception of housing as though they were fully consumed during the period in which they are purchased. Housing, because of its longevity, is treated as an 'investment' which then yields a flow of consumption services in each subsequent year to the occupiers. Apart from housing, and in some countries motor vehicles, 'investment' is used statistically to refer to durable items purchased by firms.

The relevance of this consumption/investment discussion is that it throws light on the problems which will arise in attempting to treat education in purely economic terms. In terms of practical measurement, the statistical conventions must be followed and investment restricted to those aspects of education which affect the production activities of the individual. This will not coincide with the way in which the individual would theoretically make the evaluation. The main differences between the two measures will emerge in the discussion which follows. One further difference which will arise is that for decision purposes the calculations are always made before the event, that is, it is on the basis of expectation about the costs and future returns that the individual decides whether education is worthwhile. The statistical calculations, however, will be derived from the actual experiences of different people. If everybody had perfect knowledge of the future, estimates would always be confirmed by subsequent events, but in practice this is not so, resulting in differences between the 'anticipated' and 'realised' returns on investments.

Equipped with this general exposition of the difficulties, the detailed points which arise in theory and practice may now be examined. The procedure adopted is first to examine theoretical aspects, to follow this with a review of the statistical calculations made, and then draw the discussion together in the final section.

II

For an individual, the costs of acquiring education will be considered as referring to items which entail monetary transactions, and may be thought of as falling into two categories: direct costs involving payments on the student's part, and indirect costs involving loss of receipts by him. There is also the possibility that certain non-monetary costs could arise, but for reasons which will emerge later it is more convenient if they are dealt with as part of the returns (in this case negative) on education.

Direct costs entailing payments will not relate exclusively to educational items, such as fees for courses or purchases of books and study materials, but will also cover ancillary items such as additional transport costs or living expenses. From the viewpoint of the individual investor the concept of educational cost will not be confined to any narrow definition of education such as that used in the previous chapter. While it may be difficult in practice to identify some of these direct cost items (how does one, for example, decide whether food costs will be higher and by how much, if engaged in education rather than some other activity?) they do not give rise to any conceptual problems, hence they need not be explored in any detail at this juncture.

With indirect costs on the other hand, some controversy exists as to their precise nature and the correct procedure for their treatment, hence it will be useful to consider this category in more detail. For the individual, indirect costs are usually thought of as the loss of money earnings which will occur in cases where the student would otherwise have been employed, or otherwise economically active. This loss of earnings arises because in addition to materials such as books it is also necessary for the student to devote time to the acquisition of education; and time, being a scarce resource, has various alternative uses on which a value can be placed. The question that arises is whether such costs should be included in any calculations of costs and returns from education. A related question is whether there is any difference in the impact which indirect costs may have on actual decisions, as compared with direct costs.

The argument for the inclusion of indirect costs may be summarised as follows. The decision whether or not to undergo some educational course, if taken on investment grounds, must involve a comparison between two possible life-time streams of money receipts and payments, one stream with education, the other without education. Among the differences between the two streams is that the one with education will record both payments (for the direct costs) and reduced receipts (by way of forgone earnings) during the period of education. A second difference will presumably be that this stream will also record higher receipts (increased earnings) in the post-education period, and it is these additional earnings which may (for convenience) be taken as being the return on the investment.

To decide whether this return is adequate, the potential investor will compare it with the total costs incurred during the period of education, and it will be irrelevant to him what the nature of these costs was. Whether they were direct or indirect, costs represented a loss of money which was thus not available for alternative uses. The nature of the case for inclusion of indirect costs becomes clearer if the education option is rejected. In this case the gains with the non-education stream are the immediate earnings (which would have been forgone with the education stream) and the avoidance of any direct payments for education, while the net costs are the losses of any additional future earnings which the education stream would have yielded. The choice of one stream always entails the loss of the other, and the loss is a total not a partial one, so that all of the costs and benefits associated with the rejected alternative are forgone.

Becker, who is one proponent of this viewpoint, goes on to suggest that in principle, there is no distinction needed between the two types of cost.[1] Irrespective of whether education costs £200 for example by way of either direct or indirect costs, the net position of the individual who must incur this cost is the same—his possibilities for alternative spending have been cut by £200. Becker first discusses the argument that though indirect costs should be counted, they should also be separately identified since their impact may differ from that of direct costs.[2] The main argument in support of this latter view is that young people do not find it easy to borrow funds for meeting direct costs, whereas indirect costs can be met, if necessary by reducing personal consumption. Becker rejects this argument on the grounds that the individual's net position is the same whatever the nature of the cost, and the financing difficulty is also equal for each type. Thus if an individual has an income of £1,000, and wants to take an educational course, the direct and indirect costs of which are each £200, then if he wishes to maintain his other spending at £800, he would need to borrow £200, and it is immaterial whether he says he requires this to

[1]G. Becker, *Human Capital*, New York 1964.
[2]*Ibid.*, 57.

meet the direct or the indirect costs. Becker goes on to add that the real reason behind the difficulty in borrowing is not connected with the nature of the costs but rather with the age of the borrower. On average, prospective students are young; they would experience difficulty in borrowing for any investment activity because of their youth, so that their limited borrowing power has nothing to do with education as such.

The more important issue is whether or not indirect costs should be included in any estimate of total costs. The case for their exclusion has been made by Vaizey on a number of occasions.[3] The reasons advanced by him in support of this viewpoint are first, that young people are legally prohibited from working before some specified age in virtually every country; secondly, that forgone income is not calculated for other groups such as housewives or voluntary workers when calculating national income; thirdly, that it would be necessary to adjust these costs by estimates of any benefits received by students while they are being educated; and fourthly, that if all students were to leave education and seek work, a large proportion of them would almost certainly remain unemployed, at least for some time.

The first three of these arguments (which were advanced by Vaizey in his *Economics of Education*) are discussed and rejected by Becker.[4] On the first point, Becker suggests that if forgone earnings are to be excluded because education is compulsory then direct costs should equally be excluded. Concerning the second point he states that if forgone earnings are important elsewhere in the economy, then they should be counted, but the fact that they are not, does not constitute a reason for excluding them in the case of education. For the third point he applies the same reasoning as for the first, namely if consumption benefits during education are a reason for excluding indirect costs, they are equally valid for excluding direct ones. The fourth point, the incidence of unemployment among young people, is discussed by M. J. Bowman though she is not directly

[3]See J. Vaizey, *Economics of Education*, London 1962, 42–3; *Economic Aspects of Higher Education*, O.E.C.D., Paris 1964, 51; and *International Social Science Journal*, June 1962, 625.

[4]Becker, *op. cit.*, 74.

commenting on Vaizey's advocacy of it.[5] As part of a careful discussion of the difficulties in distinguishing the 'monetary' and 'real' costs of education, she suggests that the best of the possible cost measures of student time is the earnings of those of similar age, prior training and ability, who are in employment, and she contends that no adjustment for unemployment should be made, because the intention is to measure resources, not the failure to use them.

In distinguishing between these conflicting views, one of the first points to decide is whether the problem is being viewed from the standpoint of the individual or from that of the community as a whole. Thus the introduction of compulsory education may lead to differences in the calculation of indirect costs as seen from the community as against the individual viewpoint. Any one individual might feel that in the absence of compulsion he might be able to earn a certain sum, based on his knowledge of prevailing wage rates. Whether this would be true for all individuals is not clear—Vaizey's suggestion that a mass switch to the labour force would result in greater juvenile unemployment is only part of the story. If the usual competitive conditions are met, it could be argued that such unemployment would only be temporary, and that changes in relative wage rates would enable the additional labour to be employed. Even in cases where wage-rates are rigid in a downward direction, so that this solution is not practicable, it could be contended that by the use of fiscal and other weapons, the authorities might be able to operate full employment policies. Since there is a variety of possibilities of this sort at the level of the overall economy, it is clearly not a simple matter to say what the *actual* sequence of indirect costs appropriate for any one economy at any one time would be. Moreover, there is a further complication in attempting to estimate actual forgone earnings in situations where compulsion exists, in that the calculations can be affected by other elements in the legal framework. Consider first, for example, a community which decides to extend compulsory education, and in addition

[5]M. J. Bowman, 'The Costing of Human Resource Development', in *Economics of Education*, ed., Robinson and Vaizey, London 1965.

passes legislation forbidding the employment of young people in the relevant age-group. For the individual the calculation of forgone earnings from work now becomes zero, and attendance at school becomes a choice which is made at the expense of 'leisure-time'. In contrast, in a situation where attendance at school is the only legal requirement, there could be some loss of actual earnings. The amount of this loss will be influenced by the possibilities of work at week-ends, after school hours, or during vacations, but will presumably be positive in the majority of cases where individuals would have chosen 'work' in the absence of compulsion. Clearly then the nature of the *actual* loss of earnings, which an individual experiences in situations where legal sanctions are present, cannot be thought of as taking a single, unique form but is rather a variable which can be influenced in several ways.[6] It is important to emphasise that this opens up a divergence between the nature of the individual choice and that of the community as a whole, because the individual will treat the legal and institutional framework as a datum, whereas for the community it is a variable, hence the range of choice open to the individual is more restricted.

This divergence between individual and community calculations would mean that the former would alter each time there was a change in the framework, which would both increase the difficulties of trying to make such measurements in practice and would also reduce their usefulness, since comparisons over time or between communities would be rendered more complex. This wider problem may, however, be left aside here. Given that the objective at this stage is to measure from the viewpoint of the individual, we may conclude that the existence of compulsion affects the *size* of the indirect costs which the individual will incur, but does not mean that they will be excluded from his calculations.

Similar conclusions may be applied to the question of whether the alternative to education is unemployment rather than employment. This issue is relevant at the overall com-

---

[6]Similar viewpoints have been advanced by H. Schaffer, 'Investment in Human Capital: Comment', *American Economic Review*, December 1961, and by J. Wiseman, Cost Benefit Analysis in Education', *Southern Economic Journal*, July 1965.

munity level—and will be taken up in the next chapter—but the individual will again make his calculations on the basis of the actual situation which he confronts, and would estimate his probability of obtaining work as well as the likely payment he would receive for it. In practice the problem is to obtain some acceptable basis for valuing student time since the alternative choice for many might be 'leisure' rather than work, so that Bowman's suggestion of using the earnings of those of similar age, prior training and ability who were in employment is at best only a proxy measure (as the author recognises) of the opportunity cost of time allocated to education, since all people do not have the same preferences as between work and leisure.

This whole problem of the valuation of 'leisure' time is in large part the result of a failure in conventional economic analysis formally to incorporate time into the explanation of choices as between work and leisure, work and work, leisure and leisure. An attempt to cope with this omission has been made by Becker, who demonstrates that the usual work/leisure analysis—which views the cost of the commodity called 'leisure' as being entirely composed of forgone earnings, and the cost of other commodities as being composed of goods—is only one of a set of cases.[7] More generally, virtually all of the activities in which people engage require the use of both time and goods. This means that there are two determinants of the importance of forgone earnings: the amount of time used per unit of goods, and the cost per unit of time. Hence no adequate measure of forgone earnings can be obtained by following the traditional approach and treating the production and consumption choices of people as though they were independent of each other. Instead it is necessary to allow formally for the inter-actions which occur between the two and Becker demonstrates how such an interdependent choice system can be constructed. Applying this approach to educational choices would mean that account would be taken not only of that time which is devoted to education at the expense of work, but also of that which is allocated at the expense of leisure. Becker's system explicitly illustrates that it is immaterial whether time given to

[7] G. Becker, 'A Theory of the Allocation of Time', *Economic Journal*, September 1965.

education is thought of as initially coming from either 'work' or 'leisure'; *all* time allocated will impose costs on the individuals concerned, hence will cause them to re-allocate their remaining time as between 'work' and 'leisure'. This position of Becker's is also adopted by Wiseman who, though developing the argument in a different manner, similarly concludes by arguing the necessity of including the opportunity cost of so-called 'leisure' time in any calculation of indirect costs.

But while these discussions of the opportunity cost of time help to illuminate the nature of the real choices and real costs involved in educational decisions, they do little to solve the practical problem of the valuation of time. In practice, for example, how is one to treat Wiseman's case of the boy, who in the absence of compulsion chooses to go fishing rather than work, because he values this 'leisure' activity more highly? It can be agreed that valuing this time at zero or at the prevailing wage rate will result in an understatement of its value, but no reasonable method for estimating its actual value is available. In practice, it would seem that one is forced back to using the wage-rate as the best approximation, despite its limitations. In support of this approach it could be contended that since any constraint such as compulsory education leads to a re-allocation of the remaining time available to the entire population, this will bring about changes in the wage rate until this rate once again measures the cost of *marginal* leisure time, and marginal valuation is all that can be hoped for, with any pricing system.

In addition, recalling the earlier discussion of investment and consumption, it could be contended that since rate-of-return measurements treat education as an investment activity, the prime concern when measuring opportunity costs is not necessarily to identify the actual next use of the resources in question, but rather to estimate their next best investment use. In the present instance this means that attention would focus on work, where time is used to earn a monetary return, rather than on leisure uses of time.

At this point it may be appropriate to take account of Vaizey's point that the value of any consumption benefits which students receive through being at school should also be included in the calculations. While it may be correct that such benefits should enter into the overall calculations, it is not clear that they should be treated in the manner which Vaizey suggests, namely, subtracting such benefits from the total costs in order to obtain a figure for net costs. The more usual procedure is to identify all cost and benefit items separately, rather than calculate net cost or benefits for different components of a project. Provided the calculations are carried out correctly, it ultimately makes no difference which method is used, since either method of calculation will yield the same result. The only practical relevance of the point is that it demonstrates the ubiquitous nature of costs or benefits since the same item can be entered on one side of the account as a positive, or alternatively recorded on the opposite side of the account as a negative, benefit. The usual solution adopted is to reserve the cost side for items which entail monetary payments or loss of receipts, hence this item, if admitted, would appear on the benefit side of the account.

Vaizey's approach could be justified if the initial investment costs were to be viewed as the net costs incurred during the *period* of education. However the more conventional approach with business investments is to cost them in terms of the *activity* or *item* (building a factory, purchasing a machine).

The final point raised by Vaizey, that indirect costs are not included in National Income measurements, is true, but irrelevant if one is interested in the nature of the choice which the individual or community faces when taking educational decisions. Vaizey must be aware of this, so why then does he raise the point? The explanation is probably to be found not in any theoretical elaboration, but in the more practical realm of policy decisions, since Vaizey's apparent fear is that if indirect costs are counted it will make the cost calculations for any educational scheme look very large, and will thus slow down the pace of educational advance. There may be some substance in this view, since most decision-makers are not economists and will not distinguish the separate nature of different cost categories. While, however, it may be necessary to exercise care over the manner in which results are presented to policy-makers, and Vaizey's reminder is therefore a useful one, it does not affect the nature of the calculation the individual should make, which should include his indirect costs. So far as the individual is concerned, he will not be interested in—indeed, will probably not be aware of—the way in which his activities are classified by statisticians.

To summarise this discussion of the cost aspects of education it may be said that in principle the intention is to adopt a full opportunity cost approach, that is, to compare the costs and benefits of education with the costs and benefits of the next best use which the individual could make of the same time and resources, and thereby to arrive at the net gain (or loss) associated with education. In practice we cannot measure in this way because both situations cannot co-exist, so instead we must compare what the individual actually does with some *estimate* of what he might have done. Any actual calculations must (as will be seen later) be based on comparisons of the experience of different people. At this stage, however, the concern is with the nature of people's choices as between education and other activities, and these will be made on the basis of expected future rates of return. Of the two categories of cost which were distinguished, direct costs present little conceptual difficulty. Indirect costs, that is, the costs incurred by students themselves through their having to devote time to education rather than to other activities, can give rise to some ambiguity. Hence it is necessary, when making any estimate of such indirect costs, to specify clearly the assumptions which are being made regarding the possible alternative uses of student time. It has been seen that any calculations are at best only approximate measures of these costs. The most feasible valuation method is to assume that work is the alternative to education, and therefore to use wage rates as a measure of student-time costs, though it is recognised that such an approach can lead to undervaluation of time costs in some cases.

III

The identification and measurement of benefits gives rise to problems, many of which are similar to those encountered above in the discussion of costs. In this case there will be the additional complication of distinguishing between economic and non-economic benefits. As before, there will be a range of possible benefits from the more obvious direct type to more complex and more nebulous items of an indirect nature.

The most obvious and most important form which benefits might be expected to take would be increased future earnings. Such increased earnings might be the result either of education making the individual more productive in any one occupation, or they might arise because education would qualify him for more highly paid occupations than those otherwise open to him. In practice, potential occupations and earnings will vary considerably between individuals, and will depend not only on their educational levels, but on a multiplicity of factors such as ability, sex, age, geographical location, and similar characteristics which define the range of opportunities available to the individual. No conceptual problems exist with this question of increased earning capacity; the difficulties at the practical level are formidable, since the individual will require not only a reasonable assessment of his own capabilities and characteristics, but also adequate data on the employment opportunities and earnings associated with various educational levels. The discussion of these is more appropriately postponed until the next section which deals with the statistical attempts at estimating earnings/education relationships.

Apart from the direct monetary effect on earnings, a number of indirect effects of varying importance have also been attributed to education by various authors. A convenient classification for discussion purposes is that of Weisbrod who lists four other types of benefit to the individual and three types to the remainder of society.[8] Those for the individual are the value of the option to continue with further education, the option value of wider employment possibilities, the insurance value of hedging against technological change, and fourthly, non-market benefits. The discussion of social benefits which he groups into residence-related benefits, employment-related benefits and benefits to the rest of society, will be deferred to the next chapter.

[8]B. A. Weisbrod, 'External Benefits of Public Education', *Journal of Political Economy*, October 1962.

The first option is that of continuing with subsequent education. This may be illustrated as follows. A graduate from first-level education who is deciding whether or not to study at second level would include in his calculations not only the returns which would accrue if he terminated his education at the end of second-level course, but also the value of the option which it would confer on him to proceed to third-level education. If this latter education is also a worthwhile proposition, then the option will have a positive value and should be included when counting the full returns on the second-level course. While this full opportunity-cost concept may be appropriate when considering one individual at one point in the educational pyramid, care must be taken to avoid double-counting. Thus if the individual eventually exercises his option and goes on to third-level education, then the value which he assigned to this option must be included in the costs of the third-level course. If this were not done, part of the benefits from third-level education would be counted twice, once at the point of commencing second-level education when they appear as a potential future option, and again, when third-level education is itself being assessed.

Somewhat different comments might apply to the second benefit, namely the option value of employment opportunities. Here the idea is that increased education widens the range of jobs for which the individual is qualified, and therefore he would attach a positive value to having extra job possibilities available to him. Weisbrod suggests that this approach may also be a useful way of measuring the non-monetary benefits of various occupations since by obtaining the difference between the actual earnings of an individual, and the amount which he could have earned in some other job for which he was eligible, an estimate of the value placed on the non-monetary benefits of his chosen occupation may be obtained. Thus, the argument goes, if the individual could earn £3,000 per annum, in a post which carried greater stresses, or had to be carried on in less comfortable conditions than the post he actually chooses, which carries a lower salary of £2,500, then £500 would be an estimate of the annual value which the individual placed on the non-monetary attractions of his chosen post. A first comment to make on the suggestion is that it would be extremely difficult in practice to differentiate between the monetary and the non-monetary aspects of occupations. An individual might select a lower paid job, for example, because there were lower transport or other incidental costs associated with it, so that while his gross salary might be lower, his net salary could be higher. The suggested measure of the non-monetary attractions may then be correct at the theoretical level; the practical problem would be to find some measure of *all* the monetary payments and receipts associated with various occupations.

The more important question, however, is to decide whether an option benefit of this type should be included in any 'investment' calculation of education. Some of its elements would suggest that it should, but others would seem to show it should more appropriately be excluded. Thus if possession of the option is viewed by the individual as something which itself gives satisfaction (the pleasant feeling that alternative jobs are open to him) then this 'psychic' benefit is more appropriately treated as consumption. Similarly if the option were being sought in order to give access, not to more highly-paid, but to more pleasant jobs, it would constitute a form of consumption. If on the other hand the option is regarded as something which, apart from any prospect of widening access to higher-paid jobs, also increases the degree of *certainty* attached to any given level of anticipated earnings, then it would be an 'investment' item, since lowering the degree of uncertainty raises the value of the anticipated earnings stream, and is akin to acquiring a form of insurance against unexpected reductions in earnings.

The third benefit suggested by Weisbrod—the insurance value of the hedge against technological change—gives rise to somewhat similar considerations to the employment option, and may superficially appear identical with it. The employment option, however, refers to the range of occupations available, whereas the insurance hedge refers to the premium which the individual would be prepared to pay to insure against the chance of redundancy or reduced earnings resulting from technological changes which produce adverse effects on his existing occupation. If, as is usually held, education makes workers more flexible and more readily adaptable to new skills and knowledge, then it would reduce this risk. The first question to be asked is whether this hedge is ever in fact utilised, for if it is not, then the actual value of it is zero. Data on the frequency with which jobs are changed, classified by the educational levels of the workers concerned, would be needed to throw light on this, but it may be supposed that the answer is in the affirmative. If this is so, then this insurance may be worth something to the individual. It may be noticed that the benefit of less job changing will be already included in any measure of the *actual* lifetime earnings of an individual. Hence the need for such a correction only arises in practice because calculations are generally made from statistics covering relatively short time periods. As with the previous option it might also be contended that this hedge against the need to change jobs need not necessarily refer to any *actual* monetary benefit, but to the feeling of security which the possession of the option confers, but following the reasoning of the previous paragraph such 'consumption' benefits will be excluded.

A separate point which may be worth noting regarding these insurance-type options is that they might affect the form which educational provision takes. Thus a more general education, which would provide flexibility, might also take longer than the preparation needed to qualify for one specific occupation. Were this so, there would be costs to the individual and society in providing this more general education. Attempts to determine the significance of this point would be complex, since each type of worker might have a different productivity level in given occupations. An alternative way to tackle this point might be to compare a worker who obtains a given period of 'flexible' education, with one who has an equal amount of 'specific' education. The possibility of obtaining much data of this type is complicated in practice, because people with the greatest amounts of general education also receive the greatest amounts of on-the-job (specific) training.[9] In addition, as Becker observes, the presence of specific knowledge or skills introduces an element of indeterminacy into the wage rate of its possessor, since it creates a gap between his value in one specialised activity and that in other occupations. His wage

[9]See J. Mincer, *Journal of Political Economy*, 1958 and October 1962.

rate need no longer reflect his actual productivity; it will rather depend on his bargaining position and that of his employer how close his rate is pushed to either the higher specific extreme or the lower alternative rates.

The final category of individual benefits to which Weisbrod refers are those of a non-market nature. Though difficult to identify and describe, these are nonetheless real, and may in some instances be important. Frequently they are described in general terms, such as the ability to lead a fuller life. When they are put in this form it is quite easy to become enmeshed in philosophical and similar issues, but here they will again be given a more narrow economic connotation. Weisbrod gives an interesting illustration of the significance of these non-market economic effects by quoting the example of literate individuals completing their own income tax returns. Valuing these at the level of accountants' fees shows an appreciable saving which taxpayers can make as a result of being educated. Again, however, there appear to be some difficulties with measurements of this type. Weisbrod himself notes one, namely that the alternative to self-reporting would presumably be, not the hiring of accountants, but the use by the government of some other tax. He accordingly presents an estimate of the difference in costs of collection associated with income and sales taxes (as the assumed tax alternative) as a measure of this use of literacy. This, however, is a completely different approach since it views the problem from the position of the community as a whole. For any one individual his original suggestion is more appropriate, because the tax system will be taken by him as fixed. Hence the choice in such cases is between self-completion of tax forms or having someone else perform this service. The defect with Weisbrod's valuation of this approach, however, is that he assumes the opportunity cost to the individual in preparing the return is zero, in other words that the time used has no alternative valuable use. This seems to imply an assumption of rigid working hours, which is not compatible with an assumption of a perfect market, where people could choose to work fewer or more hours as desired. It might be more appropriate then to assume that some, if not all, individuals have opportunities of substituting work for leisure, at the margin. Those who can do so at wage rates higher than accountants' fees will choose to work, and hire an accountant; it is only individuals whose marginal earning rates are below the fee rates who will complete their own tax forms. But even here it will be noted that there will be positive opportunity costs. In the absence of any more definite data on the point, it might be appropriate to value these at half the rate of fees, on the assumption that forgone earnings range from zero up to the fee level, giving an unweighted average equal to half of the fee level. (An accurate measure would call for a weighted average, that is, a knowledge of the numbers in the various earnings categories, since a simple average understates the relative importance of the more numerous groupings.)

Despite the practical difficulties of measurement, these various suggestions are useful illustrations of the way in which a comprehensive assessment of potential benefits might be undertaken by the individual. Apart from the exclusion of consumption benefits, the discussion has also omitted any reference to what are termed 'external' benefits or 'neighbourhood' effects, that is, effects on the welfare of others which result from one's activities. These more appropriately belong to the discussion of community aspects in the next chapter. Having thus considered the relevant costs and benefits from a theoretical viewpoint, some of the attempts at actual measurement may now be examined.

IV

As was seen earlier, there can be no possibility of making measurements for any one individual of the effect which education (or any other activity) had on his subsequent earnings, because this would require data not only on his actual earnings, but also on what these earnings would have been, in the absence of education. The way in which an individual could attempt to check whether his investment in education had been worthwhile, would be to compare his earnings with those of individuals who were otherwise comparable with him, but who did not possess the same educational experience.

This approach has been used in the various studies which have been made on education/earnings relationships. These studies do not, of course, use data relating to individual cases, because the range of variation in personal experiences would be very great. Instead, rerpresentative samples of the total population are generally taken, so that the results obtained typify the average experience of the various groups.

The major problem is to identify groups which are comparable in all other respects, but which differ in education. Since ultimately no two human beings are alike, this problem can never be adequately resolved. The intention in statistical studies is the more modest objective of identifying those characteristics which would have significant effects. In the case of earnings the main factors which are considered relevant, in addition to education, are age, sex, race, religion, geographical location, socio-economic group and ability.

The country for which the most comprehensive studies have been made is the United States. While it is perhaps invidious to do so, one study will be selected and commented on in some detail in order to illustrate the way in which the results are obtained. The example chosen is the study by Becker.[10] Although this also contains a detailed theoretical analysis of educational/earnings relationships, 'the original aim of this study was to estimate the money rate of return to college and high-school education in the United States'.[11]

The data for this study were mainly derived from the population censuses of 1940 and 1950, supplemented by a number of sample surveys, these latter dating mainly from the 1950s. The estimates are thus based on cross-section data, that is they refer to different people at the same point in time, whereas ideally we would require cohort data, that is data dealing with the same group of people throughout their working lives. This cross-section approach, however, also raised some extra problems which would not have arisen with

[10]Becker, *Human Capital*, New York 1964.
[11]*Ibid.*, 7.

the cohort approach and it may be convenient to dispose of these first.

One problem was the need to make some adjustment for the fact that not all of those who receive education will survive to the age of 65 (the usual age at which labour-force earnings data terminate). To assume that they did, would be to overstate the estimated returns which on average would be obtained from educating the young. A correction was accordingly made to calculate the proportion who would die at each age.

A second statistical adjustment was needed to allow for the probability that the rate of unemployment at the particular point in time would be different to that which would prevail over a working life. Thus the 1940 census (containing 1939 earnings data) related to a period when unemployment was high; to have taken this as being typical would have under-stated the lifetime earnings which would accrue to each group. A correction was made by calculating what would have been the earnings for each educational group if nobody had been unemployed. This probably understates the return to education, because unemployment even in more 'normal' times is usually higher among the less educated. However, since the effect this correction had on the overall results was very small, the inaccuracy was not felt to be important.

A third adjustment was needed to allow for the probability that earnings would not remain static over a working lifetime, but would show a significant rise. Not all of the observed increase in earnings over time can be used in making these corrections because, as Becker notes, much of this growth resulted from the increase in education itself. Hence it is the growth in earnings attributable to other factors which is required. In the absence of any detailed data Becker assumes that the figure is $1\frac{1}{4}$ per cent per person per annum in real terms. This raises the absolute level of lifetime earnings for each educational group. More important is the relative rate of increase for each group since it is this which influences the rate of return on any given educational level. By assuming the same percentage increase for each category, Becker is increasing the estimated rate-of-return because (as he points out elsewhere) the same percentage increase will mean a greater absolute amount to the higher-paid group, who are also the more highly educated. These larger absolute amounts will in turn raise the ratio of returns to costs, thus increasing the calculated rate-of-return.

One further adjustment which was made was a correction for changes in tax rates. Thus while the gross earnings of an educated person might show a certain increase over time, his net earnings would record a smaller rise, if income taxes had been raised during the period. For the U.S. Becker indicates that income tax accounted for about 1·5 per cent of 1939 incomes but it rose to 7·5 and 10 per cent for 1949 and 1956 respectively. Two calculations were therefore made; one using the 1939 tax rates, the second using 1949 rates in order to estimate the effects which tax changes had on private rates-of-return.

From these adjustments the calculated stream of earnings for each educational group was derived. The second step was to calculate the costs of education. Direct private costs (fees, books etc.) for college education were obtained from several special studies. High school education tuition costs (fees) were taken as zero, while other direct costs were taken as being one-half of the level calculated for college students.

Indirect costs in the form of income forgone by both college and high school students were in each case calculated by assuming that as students they earned only one-quarter of the amount earned by young people of comparable age and education who are in the labour-force full time. Becker discusses the results of surveys and other estimates which suggest that these assumptions are quite reasonable.

The rates-of-return (the process described at the beginning of this chapter, or, more precisely in the present case, the discount rate which will reduce to zero the difference in earnings between the educational levels in question) for the various groups were then calculated. In the case of college education, he presents a range of estimates for the 1939 male, white urban graduates, applying different income-tax rates, and varying assumptions about the long-term growth in earnings, which show rates-of-return from 13 to almost 17 per cent, and gives 14·5 per cent as the best single estimate for this group.

The interpretation of these, and of the other rates to be quoted, is that they represent the net return which a high school graduate could expect to earn on the costs of obtaining a college education. Estimates for all male whites graduating in 1949 yield a figure of 13 per cent as the best single estimate. Since the two sets of estimates are not directly comparable (apart from the 1949 data covering all, and not just urban graduates, they also relate to total income, whereas the 1939 data was for estimated earnings), no significance should be attached to the difference between the two sets of estimates.

Calculations of rates-of-returns for other groups are also presented. In the case of non-white males these range from 6·6 to 14 per cent for the 1939 cohort, with best estimates of 12·3 for those in the south and 8·3 per cent for the north. No direct estimates are presented for females, though reference is made to other studies which calculate lower rates-of-return for them. In the case of high school education, estimates are presented for 1939 and 1949 white males on the same basis as for college groups. The best estimates emerge as 16 per cent for the 1939 and 20 per cent for the 1949 cohort.

These estimates are of course based on the *total* difference in earnings between college and high school graduates in the various categories, but as was seen earlier, not all of these differences can be attributed to education. Some of the factors which were listed there, namely age, sex and race, are accounted for in these estimates. Of the remaining factors, religion is not discussed by Becker. Location is dealt with briefly in a reference to the differences recorded for rural dwellers from which it appears that both income differentials and indirect costs are lower as compared with urban areas, but no specific rates-of-return are calculated. The remaining factors discussed are those of ability and on-the-job training, and Becker examines the possible effect which these, especially ability, might have on the observed income differences. Becker first notes that there are differences in ability between those who graduate from college and those who do not, and draws on the results of various studies which used different methods of measurement in order to estimate the impact of this factor. One of these was a study of the earnings of brothers who had had different amounts of education. This may reasonably be discarded since differences in ability, though not perhaps as great as those which would exist for the population as a whole, are nonetheless likely to be present, hence the estimate would not be free of ability influences.

A second study used data on earnings for Bell Telephone Company which indicated that while starting salaries were not greatly affected by rank in class, after fifteen years in employment those who had been in the top two-fifths of their college class earned about 20 per cent more than those who had been in the bottom two-fifths. Using this as a basis, the rate-of-return for a typical high school graduate completing college would be about two per cent lower than the 14.5 per cent for actual graduates since the latter contain a greater proportion of above-average people. A third estimate was based on a study of data for 2,800 high school graduates.[12] This showed earnings classified by rank in high school and by education (college degree, some college, or high school). For each educational group those who had ranked higher in high school earned more than those ranked lower (and, as expected, those with more education earned more than those with less). The rank-adjusted rate-of-return derived from this is similar to that shown by the Bell data. This study also contains data on the fathers' occupation which indicate that allowing for this factor alone would hardly affect the gain of a typical college graduate and would reduce the rate-of-return from college to a typical high school graduate by about one percentage point. A fourth estimate is provided by a study using multiple regression techniques to calculate the effects on family earnings of white male heads of non-farm households in the labour force, accounting for religion, personality, fathers' occupation, labour market conditions, mobility and supervisory responsibilities.[13] In total these factors explained about 40 per cent of the differential in the 18–34 age group and 12 per cent in the 35–74 age group. Hence education itself was again left as the main explanatory

[12]D. Wolfe and J. Smith, 'The Occupational Value of Education for Superior High School Graduates', *Journal of Higher Education*, April 1956.

[13]J. Morgan and M. David, 'Education and Income', *Quarterly Journal of Economics*, August 1963.

factor of the difference. Becker does not calculate what the net effect of those figures would be on his rate-of-return, but at the outside they would hardly reduce it by more than 3 percentage points. His final estimate of the effect of ability is based not on graduates but on data for college drop-outs which show that though the ability of these drop-outs appears to be lower than that of college graduates, and comparable with that of high school graduates, the rates-of-return were 9·5 and 8 per cent on this college education for the 1939 and 1949 cohorts. Becker suggests it is reasonable to expect that the gain from completing a course would be greater than that for only completing a portion of it, hence the rates for graduates should be higher than those for drop-outs. Summarising all of these varying studies Becker concludes that while the rates-of-return should be reduced from the original levels of 14·5 and 13 per cent in order to allow for the contribution of ability, they may still be taken as being greater than 10 per cent for white male college graduates.

The final possible influence on earnings which Becker considers is that of other forms of human investment such as on-the-job training. Having noted the paucity of data on these aspects he concludes that on theoretical grounds there is no reason to expect that they would produce any significant difference in the calculated rates-of-return.

Apart from this study by Becker, various other estimates have been made of the rates-of-return to education in the U.S. It is not necessary to discuss these here, however, because despite differences in data, methods and assumptions, they are sufficiently similar to Becker's work to be counted as part of the same basic group. In particular, there is unanimity in the conclusion, that for the U.S. in recent decades, education pays.

No comparable studies are available for other countries, due partly, no doubt, to the absence of comparable statistical data. It may be of interest to note the results of two studies for the U.K. based on sample data. The first of these used details from a sample of 6,500 male heads of households aged 20 and over, which gave information on income and the age at which full-time education was completed.[14] No details were available,

[14]M. Blaug, *The Money Rate-of-Return on Education in the U.K.*, Manchester School, September 1965.

however, on ability or other factors which might have influenced earnings. In the absence of such information the proportions which Becker had calculated for the U.S. were applied. Accordingly 60 per cent of the observed differences in income were attributed to education and the remaining 40 per cent to the influence of other factors. On this basis the estimated private rates-of-return for the 1963 cohort, were 10 per cent for the three years of upper secondary school and 14 per cent for three years university education. It may be noted that making the adjustment for ability etc., on the American basis, was felt on balance to result probably in some under-statement of the true rate for university level and some over-statement of that for secondary education, because factors such as ability and social class are of greater relative importance at second-level education in the British system.

The second British study was based on data for about 3,000 employees of five firms, mainly in the electrical engineering industries.[15] Their earnings were related to age and educational level, the latter being grouped into seven categories, ranging from no qualifications beyond school-leaving age up to honours and post-graduate university degrees. Using the same cross-section method as Becker, the lifetime earnings associated with each educational level were derived, and from these, the apparent rates-of-return to each educational level were then estimated. In relation to the base level of education used (no qualifications beyond school-leaving age, plus education level unknown) the six higher educational levels yielded private rates-of-return ranging from 7 to $11\frac{1}{2}$ per cent (including 2 per cent per annum as the estimated long-run growth in income per head). The incremental rates-of-return between various educational levels were also estimated. An honours degree or higher qualification, for example, yielded almost 11 per cent over G.C.E. 'A' level or equivalent education, whereas a pass degree showed a return of about $8\frac{1}{2}$ per cent. Both G.C.E. 'A' level, or 'O' level qualifications in turn yielded about 8 per cent over the base educational group.

[15]M. Blaug, M. Peston and A. Ziderman, *The Utilisation of Educated Manpower in Industry*, Edinburgh 1967.

No attempt was made to adjust these estimates for the impact of ability or other non-educational influences on earnings. Much lower rates-of-return would be obtained for this study, for example, if the 40 per cent correction factor used in the earlier study were applied. However, there is again no direct significance to be read into the difference in rates-of-return. The second study was not only concerned with a much narrower segment of the total population (effectively employees in one industry) which might be expected to show a smaller range of differences, it was in addition confined to earnings as distinct from total income. Moreover, since the base educational category used contained those whose education was unknown, it is possible that the earnings of those with minimal educational levels were overstated, and hence the incremental earnings on the higher levels understated.

Taken in conjunction, these two British studies show that rates-of-return would appear to be significantly above zero and could well lie in the range where education would constitute an attractive investment to the economically motivated individual. As such they are similar to the general results of the various U.S. studies.

In addition to these studies of the relationship between education and earnings, it may also be of interest to note the results of attempts made by Weisbrod to quantify some of the indirect economic benefits, which were outlined in the previous section. Of the four types of 'option' suggested, no attempt was made to estimate the value of either the 'employment' option (the wider range of job opportunities created by education) or the technological 'hedge' option (reducing the risk of unemployment created by technological changes). Of the 'non-monetary' effects, Weisbrod estimates the values of self-completion of income-tax assessments at $250 million.[16] He regards the ability to perform this task as a function of literacy and hence most appropriately treated as a return on elementary rather than on higher levels of education. From the data used by him, this return was in the region of 3 per cent.

[16]B. A. Weisbrod, 'Education and Investment in Human Capital', *Journal of Political Economy* (supplement), October 1962.

Estimates are also given of the 'education' option (the opportunity which completion of one educational level creates for proceeding to higher levels). As noted in the earlier discussion care is needed in the interpretation of such option values, otherwise the return on a higher educational level might be counted twice. In order to avoid any 'double-counting' problems Weisbrod presents illustrative calculations which include only a portion of the potential return on higher levels in estimating the value of the option at the point of entering the lower educational level. Using data from Schultz he takes the rates-of-return on high school level as 14 per cent, on a college degree as 9 per cent, and on partial completion of college as 8 per cent, and then shows how the value of this option for college education might be valued for a student about to enter high school.[17] He assumes that the funds needed to buy college education at the later date could, if invested elsewhere, yield 5 per cent. Thus the increased yield to be obtained from completing college would be 4 per cent (9 per cent – 5 per cent) while that for partially completing a college course would be 3 per cent (8 per cent – 5 per cent).

To calculate the value of these incremental returns in terms of the return on high school education, two further adjustments are needed. The first is to correct for differences in the cost of college and high school education. In these calculations, the costs of a college degree course are taken as 2·7 times those of a high school course, hence a rate-of-return of 4 per cent on the costs of college education is equivalent to one of 10·8 per cent on those of a high school education. The second correction deals with the probability of a high school graduate actually going on to take a college degree. Since not all high school graduates do so, ignoring this problem would overstate the option's value. The data used by Weisbrod show 24 per cent as the proportion of high school graduates who completed college; by applying this factor to the 10·8 per cent figure the final value of this part of the option becomes 2·6 per cent.

Similar calculations are made for the value of partial college

[17]T. W. Schultz, 'Education and Economic Growth', in *Social Forces Influencing American Education*, National Society for the Study of Education. Chicago 1961.

education, which yield a final value of 0·8 per cent, giving a combined value of the option for college education of 3·4 per cent. Taking this option into account would thus raise the rate-of-return on high school education from 14 per cent to 17·4 per cent. A second set of calculations for elementary education (for which the initial rate-of-return is again taken from Schultz) shows the value of the option for high school education as almost 14 per cent and for college education as 5 per cent, raising the overall rate-of-return on this level of education from 35 per cent to 54 per cent. The value of the option is naturally greater, the lower the educational level being considered, since it will be obvious that at the highest educational level, where no further course is possible, the option must have a zero value.

These quantitative estimates of the possible values which some of the options created by education may assume are of some interest since they show that the amounts involved are relatively large, and hence could affect the individual's decision whether or not to 'buy' any one educational course.

V

Having now considered both the theoretical and empirical aspects of rate-of-return studies, it remains to dispose of some unsettled points and to decide the relevance of these studies to the patterns of private demand for education.

It is not proposed to discuss the accuracy or validity of the various studies, since the authors themselves are the first to point out the statistical difficulties and practical limitations on their efforts. Neither is it necessary to review the treatment of the various factors other than education which may have influenced earnings, since these have already been discussed in some detail. At this stage the intention is rather to ask what interpretation, if any, could be placed on such estimates, and whether any further information would increase their value.

One aspect to emphasise is that the studies have so far been considered in terms of average results. These however do not reveal anything of the range of variation which can occur between individuals. Becker presents some data to show that these variations can be significant. While the average rate-of-return on college education was, say, 12 per cent, more than one-third of the group in question would have estimated rates which either exceeded 24 per cent or were below zero. Such a range of variation in the results could clearly influence the individual's decision, but it did not appear that there was much the individual could do to reduce the range of uncertainty by acquiring additional information beforehand. The known risks which he might anticipate such as sex, race, and geographical location did not in themselves appear to 'explain' much of the earnings differentials, so that the bulk of the variations would still remain. Even differences in ability, which might be anticipated to some extent (though this is somewhat doubtful since young people are unlikely to be fully informed regarding their talents) are apparently not of much significance, at least at college level.

A major source of this individual uncertainty, in Becker's view, is the long pay-back period for educational investment. Even though the overall lifetime return might work out at the equivalent of 12 or 13 per cent per annum, the U.S. data showed that the investment had not repaid its cost ten years after graduation. This is in marked contrast to business investment, which typically pays back its costs in five years or less. The reason for the long pay-back period in education is that the earnings differentials associated with education are much smaller for the younger, than for the older, age-groups. For example, in the study of U.K. firms noted earlier, the sample data showed that the average earnings of those in the base-level group were £967, £1,166 and £1,226 for the age-groups 25–29, 35–39 and 45–49 respectively, whereas those with G.C.E. 'A' level or equivalent were £1,011, £1,343, and £1,603, while those for the highest group (honours university degree or equivalent) were £1,249, £2,198 and £2,709 for the same age-groups. Hence while the more highly educated had higher earnings at each age by comparison with their less educated counterparts, the actual size of the earnings gap was very much greater for the older age-groups. This long pay-back period implies that the investor in education needs to take a much more long-term view than the average business investor.

A further factor relevant for individual decision-making would be the behaviour of marginal, as distinct from average, rates-of-return, that is, the returns which additional people possessing any one educational level could expect to earn. If the demand for labour remained unchanged, for example, the normal expectation would be for an increase in the supply of people possessing a given educational qualification leading to a reduction in the wages or salary which they could command; so the marginal rate-of-return for new entrants would be below the average rate earned by the initial members of the group. More realistically, changes in rates-of-return over time will occur in response to changes in educational demand and supply and in response to labour force demand and supply.

Finally, it is worth noting that any consumption benefits derived from education are excluded. In itself this is reasonable when considering an activity from an investment viewpoint, since the consumption benefits of alternative investment opportunities will likewise be excluded from any statistical calculation.

This last factor may however complicate any attempt to interpret the results of rate-of-return data. Thus, if it were observed that returns on educational investment were lower than those on alternative investments, this position might be rationalised by saying that the various consumption benefits of education were sufficient to offset the difference. If the reverse case applied, the high rates-of-return could be explained in terms of the consumption benefits of alternative investments. A different explanation, however, would be to use high rates-of-return on education as indicators of shortages, and low rates as showing surpluses of educated people. Thus, a rise in the rate-of-return to some category, say engineers, associated with supply rising less rapidly than the demand can be interpreted as defining a relative shortage of engineers. The difference between these two explanations is that the first is more appropriate to a static equilibrium description, and the second to dynamic disequilibrium situations. In other words the former would be appropriate to a situation in which the conditions of a competitive market economy were fully satisfied so that consumers were always in their chosen situation. The second explanation seeks to describe the process by which consumers adjust through time to changes which were imperfectly, or perhaps were even completely unforeseen. The emergence of a shortage, for example, would be eventually expected to lead to an expansion of supply, which would then cause rates-of-returns to stabilise or fall. The presence of consumption benefits, however, would not make it possible to identify any equilibrium position. If, moreover, the value of these consumption benefits were to change over time then they would likewise bring about shifts in relative rates-of-return. While it is always possible to discuss movements in rates-of-return in terms of these static and dynamic elements, it is not easy to use this type of analysis for predictive purposes. In other words, the ability to explain historical rate-of-return data does not necessarily help in predicting future trends.

It is, however, the future trends which are of relevance to the potential investor, who seeks to estimate whether an investment now will pay back in the future. While the historical studies are undoubtedly a useful piece of information helping in the formulation of his estimates, they are not in themselves sufficient for this purpose. But apart from the perspectives which the availability of data may provide, there is a second valuable function which rate-of-return studies can perform for the individual who is interested in education, namely the educational function of showing the manner in which an investment type appraisal should be made. The range of benefits which education may confer, and their likely monetary value, are unlikely to be readily apparent to the majority of people. The making of inaccurate or inadequate assessments could result in some potential investors underestimating and to others, overestimating the return on education. A wider appreciation of the factors involved, could then help to produce a more accurate set of investment decisions on the part of economically-motivated people.

The wider policy implications which rate-of-return studies might have, on public sector activities for example, will be deferred to a later chapter. The purpose of the present chapter has been first, to show the manner in which the individual might be expected to view education from an economic viewpoint, and secondly to illustrate the rates-of-return which, the available data suggest, have been obtainable on education in the recent past. These latter rates were on average higher than the rates of interest which prevail for many sectors of the economies concerned, and thus were consistent with the hypothesis that education could be regarded as a worthwhile investment at the individual level (which is not to attribute this as the actual motivation for acquiring education). There is in consequence some justification for seeking to explore more fully the economic aspects of educational activities.

CHAPTER 4

EDUCATION AS A SOCIAL INVESTMENT

THE discussion of the previous chapter centred on the economic benefits which the individual himself might obtain from education. In addition to these, it is possible that other sections of the community—members of the same family, neighbours, work colleagues or the community in general through governmental agencies—may experience economic side-effects from the education of some of its members. Such wider consequences would be relevant to any decisions on educational spending taken by many agencies, such as government, and therefore they should be evaluated in a similar manner to the private benefits. A wider approach along these lines will now be employed, treating education in economic terms, giving rise in this instance to a need for some identification and measurement of the community-wide costs and benefits associated with education.

This wider type of approach can be considered as one form of the cost-benefit method of analysis which has been applied on a growing scale to various areas of governmental expenditure in recent decades. Since the object with these analyses is to evaluate the consequences of projects in monetary terms, so far as is possible, the methods of appraisal will be closely analogous to those used by the individual investor. They will not, however, be identical. Apart from the greater practical difficulties of identifying effects on a community-wide basis, there are also increased problems of placing monetary valuations on these effects. One main reason for these added problems is that a greater proportion of the effects are unlikely to be reflected in market transactions. Valuations in these cases must in consequence depend on more extended and more approximate methods of assessment and imputation. In cases where the

76

effect in question is so general or so pervasive in nature, situations will arise where—as will be seen later—one must question the possibility or validity of any valuation. Assuming for the present that some set of costs and benefits can be identified, the objective will be, as before, to calculate the rates-of-return involved. In order to distinguish these wider estimates from those of private investors, the results so obtained are termed 'social' rates-of-return.

With education, as with other areas where people are the subject of the potential investment, there may be some value in distinguishing within the total result the portion which accrues to the individual and that which goes to other sections of the community. The 'social' rate-of-return is an overall calculation which includes the costs and benefits to all groups, including the individuals who are being educated. As such, a rate-of-return, of say 10 per cent, could be composed of a much larger positive return to the individual, and a smaller, perhaps negative, rate to the remainder of the community. Since governments, in particular, are interested in the distributional aspects of their activities, and undertake many programmes for this reason, information on its distribution may be as relevant as data on the extent of any 'social' rate-of-return to education or similar programmes.

With this brief preamble as a basis, the re-examination of the economic aspects of education may now commence. The same sequence will be retained, first, a general discussion of the costs and benefits components, secondly, a review of some empirical studies in this field, and a final section which summarises the relevance of this approach.

II

Costs may again be split into their direct and indirect components. As in the private case, direct costs for the society as a whole present little conceptual difficulty. In a community where the total costs of education were borne by the students themselves and where the conditions for a perfectly competitive market were fulfilled, so that no divergence existed between the money cost and the real opportunity cost of the resources (other than student time) used in education, these direct costs would be merely the sum of the payments made by individual students. In practice this is not the case; divergences between real and money costs do occur, and in addition much of the costs are met, not by the students themselves, but by various forms of financial aid from the public sector, or from private agencies. In the case of direct teaching resources, pupil fees, for example, are frequently non-existent, or else they cover only a small portion of the total costs of operating the educational establishments concerned. For other items such as books, transport or maintenance expenses it is again frequently the case that cash grants are made to students towards the cost of these items, or they may be enabled to buy them at subsidised prices. These problems of actual measurement need not detain us at this stage since they are primarily of a statistical rather than of a general nature.

With indirect costs on the other hand, problems of this sort do exist, as is evident from the discussion of chapter three. It was then seen that, for the individual, these indirect costs can be valued on the basis of the extra earnings which he could have obtained by working rather than by going to school or college. For the economy as a whole the corresponding measure to this would be the loss of output which results when people study rather than work.

If the 'full' opportunity cost-approach discussed in the preceding chapter is adopted, however, there will not necessarily be a complete correspondence between the individual's calculation of indirect costs, based on his forgone earnings, and the social calculation, based on value of output forgone. As pointed out in the earlier discussion, one reason for this is that the 'full' (or social) opportunity cost-approach measures in terms of the 'potential' losses, not the expected actual losses of output. Thus, if there is a legal prohibition on work before the age of 15, the loss of earnings for a 14-year-old staying in a school will be calculated by him as zero. For a community estimate on the other hand, they would be the estimated value of the output which could be produced were the law to be removed. This method of social valuation may at first glance appear strange—it would seem to call for placing an estimate on the output lost through having even the youngest children at school (it would, if young children were to work in the absence of restrictions).

A consideration of another of the examples used earlier, that of unemployment, may however serve to clarify the logic of this full opportunity cost. Consider some young people who are contemplating college, and whose estimate of forgone earnings is lowered because there is widespread unemployment among people in their age/qualification group. In this case their estimate takes account of the probability of finding work (e.g. if the probability of a job is 80 per cent, and the pay is £500, they will calculate forgone earnings as being on average £400 per head). The full opportunity cost calculation will use £500 as the figure for loss of output, as being the potential alternative use of the students' time. The failure to realise this potential loss in full because of unemployment, does not alter the fact that this potential does represent the real cost involved and indeed serves to draw attention to the real costs of unemployment. This could in turn spur the authorities into doing something about the unemployment position, whereas valuing in terms of the actual loss of output could lead to complacency. While calculation of the actual loss of output may be helpful for short-run decisions, or for choosing the timing of some change (ignoring other aspects, for example, it would be easier to raise the school leaving age when unemployment among the young was high), the full opportunity cost measure is the more appropriate general measure. It serves to draw attention to the continuing costs of all activities, whether they be school attendance and child employment laws, or youth employment programmes. The use of the full opportunity cost measure has the added advantage of yielding comparable measures over time: in contrast to actual measurements, which would alter with circumstances. Thus to continue with the example of a change in the law concerning youth employment: actual measurement of forgone earnings would be lower following the introduction of such legislation, than would be the case for the earlier periods. A full opportunity cost measure would, on the other hand, show similar earnings and output losses in both periods.

One further point to be noted before concluding the discussion of indirect costs is the proper treatment of any change in consumption patterns which may be associated with the decision to become a student rather than enter employment. It is likely that many young persons who forgo employment may cut their consumption spending as a consequence of this fall in income. Since this cut in consumption will represent reduced demands by them on the output of the community, the suggestion has been made that the appropriate measure of indirect costs in these cases is the reduction in earnings, minus the reduction in consumption.[1] The counter-argument is that any cut in consumption is a real cost and real reduction in the welfare of the student, and hence should be counted.[2] As with many of the points raised, the difference here is again largely one of the classification used. No one would dispute that the cut in consumption is a real cost to the student, hence it would be included in his own calculation. From the community viewpoint if the definition used includes the student himself, the earnings measure is again the correct one, because the fall in the student's consumption will represent a loss to him. But his loss will be an equivalent gain to the rest of the community, so that in aggregate they cancel each other out, leaving the output (earnings) reduction as the measure of loss. Only where one was considering the community excluding the student would the fall in his consumption appear as a gain to offset against the loss of his output. Once the unit under discussion is specified, no problem need arise with the treatment of changes in consumption associated with income changes.

Finally, it may be noted that no reference has been made to any 'external' costs which may be associated with education, that is with costs which fall on persons other than those being educated. It will be more convenient to discuss all of these

---

[1]B. A. Weisbrod, 'Education and Investment in Human Capital', *Journal of Political Economy* (supplement), October 1962.
[2]M. Blaug, *Money Rate-of-Return on Education in the U.K.*, Manchester School, September 1965.

external aspects in the section on benefits, where such costs
would appear as 'negative benefits'.

III

The measurement of benefits from the community aspect
likewise introduces some additional considerations which do not
arise at the individual level. At the community level, the direct
benefits are taken as being the increment in the individual's
output which results from additional education. Apart from
the influences on output and earnings other than education
discussed in the previous chapters, such as ability, sex, location
and so forth, there are two further complications which have
now to be taken into account. One of these concerns the
treatment of tax payments by the individual. If, for example,
education is expected to raise the individual's output, and with
it, his salary by £1,000, but he is liable for income tax of 25
per cent, then he will base his calculations on the net return of
£750. A divergence between the private and social valuation of
his additional output thus arises. For calculation of social rates-
of-return, the gross value of the incremental output is used,
because this represents the total gain to the community from
his education. The payment of tax means the individual himself does not capture the whole of this increment. A question
which may present itself is whether indirect tax payments on
the goods and services which the individual purchases with his
additional (net) income should not be treated in the same way.
To do so, however, would constitute double-counting, because
the individual will have included such indirect tax payments as
part of the returns to him. To count them also as a gain to the
community would be using indirect taxes in two separate
accounts. While then the presence of indirect taxes does not
require any adjustment when moving from private to social
calculations of the absolute returns on education, such taxes
will be relevant to a consideration of the way in which the
additional output is distributed between the various groups, and
will later arise in this context.

The second possible adjustment relates to the question of

whether earnings are an adequate reflection of individual output or whether divergences between the two may arise. Bowen for example refers to the possibilities of earnings being affected by 'conspicuous production' or being 'tradition bound', the first referring to the possibility that employers may hire, say college graduates, and pay the higher salaries associated with them for jobs which could be filled satisfactorily by lesser qualified personnel.[3] The second refers to a phenomenon which is sometimes ascribed to developing countries where high salaries may continue to be paid to certain groups for tradition or status reasons after the need for such salaries may have disappeared.

This question of the extent to which imperfections occur in the determination of wages and salaries is one which has been discussed by several writers without any precise conclusion being drawn.[4] As Blaug observes, however, the main question is not whether general imperfections exist, but rather whether those imperfections exist which are 'directly related to the education received by members of the labour force', since these are the only ones which really matter when calculating educational returns.[5] Blaug suggests that if trade unions, for example, are able by their bargaining power to raise wage rates for their members above those of non-unionised groups that this would probably not affect calculations of educational returns, because they would not be among the more highly-educated groups. In contrast if employers are hiring highly-paid graduates for jobs which do not need their skill, then the returns to education would be overstated from the community viewpoint, since graduates would be receiving earnings in excess of the value of their output. Blaug, like Bowen, suggests that since these latter cases are unlikely to be so frequent as is sometimes thought, the amounts involved are not likely to be such as would invalidate any rates-of-return calculations.

The real situation however, could be more complex than these remarks suggest since it would depend on other aspects of

[3]W. G. Bowen, 'Assessing the Economic Contribution of Education' in *Economic Aspects of Higher Education*, O.E.C.D., Paris 1964, 177–200.
[4]M. Blaug, *op. cit.*, 201–5 and references there cited.
[5]*Ibid.*, 230.

the economic environment. Thus, if a less educated but highly unionised segment of workers are able to secure wage increases for themselves, and the government operates a full employment policy which results in all of them being employed, then there will be a redistribution of income in their favour. This will have the effect of lowering the observed rate-of-return on education since it will narrow wage differentials among the more highly educated groups. The reverse possibility could also occur: Blaug, for example, refers to a study which suggests that some of the earning power of the U.S. medical profession may be the result of restrictive practices on their part and, if correct, this theory would overstate the value of their education from a community viewpoint. It seems possible then that different segments of the labour force are characterised by varying degrees of monopolistic power or other imperfections which lead to divergences between their earnings and the social value of their output. What is needed to resolve this issue is data for groups with varying amounts of education, in order to determine which groups are on balance the beneficiaries from market imperfections. In the absence of such data there is no way of deciding whether observed returns to each group are correct, whether they are an overstatement or an understatement.

The existence of these imperfections may be noted, but it is not possible to say whether positive or negative correction is needed when seeking to calculate the social value of output, as distinct from the individual earnings associated with varying educational levels.

The more difficult category of benefits to identify and measure are those which accrue, not to the individual, but to other members of the community. Such effects are usually termed 'externalities' or 'neighbourhood' effects, the object being to emphasise that individual behaviour affects other members of the society. Such 'neighbourhood' effects can affect either the production or consumption activities of others, and may be of a positive (benefits) or a negative (costs) nature. Many forms of economic activity have been suggested as giving rise to these effects and there is an extensive literature dealing with their economic implications and consequences.

Education is considered as being one area which may give

rise to several forms of 'neighbourhood' effect. By way of opening the discussion it may be convenient to adopt the framework used by Weisbrod, who in addition to his discussion of the various direct and indirect benefits to the individual, also presents a useful classification of externalities into residence-related benefits, employment-related benefits and benefits to the rest of society.

An example of a residence-related benefit would be the child care service which a school provides in the case of younger children. This effect could take the form of a consumption benefit to mothers in that they might enjoy increased leisure time or reduced anxiety as a consequence of their children attending school. There could also be an economic benefit attached to the service, in that it may enable many mothers to work, who might otherwise find it uneconomic to pay for baby-sitting services during their absence at work.

A second example of such benefits would be those which accrue to the future family of the educated; the idea here being that educated parents provide informal education for their children which is of positive benefit to the latter. Weisbrod suggests that the magnitude of this might be measured by relating scores on educational achievement tests to parental education, having adjusted for variations in ability. These differences in achievement for children of given ability would then be translated into equivalent years of school attendance, to which a value (that of educational cost) could be assigned. It is not clear, however, what significance should be attached to this calculation. It may be said to overstate the benefit value since it is not likely that parents (or the community) will show any saving on actual costs, because the children will be in school for the same length of time. The effect is rather in the differential attainment of pupils for a given period; this effect is therefore likely to show itself in the differential earnings of students with different backgrounds. Hence an alternative possibility of measurement might be to allocate a proportion of the earnings attributed to educational attainment, or rank in class, to this parental effect. The proportion to be attributed would be determined by measuring the effect which parental education had on rank in class or attainment.

Weisbrod later suggested a different method of valuing the benefits which children derive from educated parents. This draws on data (discussed in chapter two) which showed that the amount of education children received was greater, the greater the educational level of the parents themselves. Assuming that parents were interested in the future well-being of their children, this data could be used to derive the additional income which the child would enjoy from his higher educational level, and then to treat this incremental income of the child as a return on the cost of the parents' education.

The third example of a residence-related benefit given by Weisbrod, refers to effects on neighbours. These may gain from the education of children in two ways; firstly the short-run benefit in that school provides children with an alternative to their own unsupervised activities, some at least of which are likely to have adverse effects on neighbours, and secondly the more long-run benefit in that educated people may develop social values which have positive beneficial effects on their neighbours. Weisbrod suggests that some indication of the presence of such effects might be obtained by studying the voting behaviour on school issues of non-parents. The inference here is presumably that if these effects are positive, neighbours will support school programmes even though they themselves are not directly concerned. A possible alternative method of measurement arises with Weisbrod's fourth example, namely the benefits to local taxpayers which may accrue from education. If, for example, lack of education leads to increased unemployment and crime, then taxpayers will be faced with the need to pay for the consequences of these problems. The social benefits which education confers may therefore be valued in terms of the reduced incidence of these costs.

The second group of social benefits are those termed 'employment-related'. Here the basic idea is that educating some workers raises the productivity of others. Weisbrod suggests that the importance of this effect depends on education developing the properties of flexibility and adaptability since it is these qualities which redound to the advantage of other workers in cases where production involves the co-operative effort of a group.

In the third residual category of effects on society in general, Weisbrod refers as an example to the effect which research activities may have on the level of output per person. This point is briefly dealt with, Weisbrod remarking on our ignorance on the topic. It does, however, seem reasonable to expect that insofar as research activities prove beneficial to society, they are a means of increasing output per worker, whether they are achieved through the introduction of new products, new production methods or through more indirect measures such as improvements in health or working conditions. Though not a return on education as such, these beneficial effects would not be possible unless research workers had first received the necessary education to form the basis for their advances.

Other effects accruing to society in general to which Weisbrod refers are items such as the value of literacy in spreading information, which is valuable both for the functioning of a market economy and for a political democracy. The impact of education in changing income distribution or providing equality of opportunity, may be explicit social goals. Again, however, these are effects which are well-nigh impossible to quantify, though this does not imply they are unimportant.

This list of examples could be extended. Many writers have endorsed and illustrated the theme that education, in the words of the Robbins Report, 'furnishes perhaps the most conspicuous example of the importance in social analysis of the difference between what economists call the "private" and the "social" net product of investment.'[6]

It is not proposed to discuss the question of 'externalities' in detail at this juncture, since this aspect is one which will also recur in later chapters. It is, however, necessary to define the extent to which externalities should enter into any calculations of the social returns to investment. The concept can be so far-reaching and pervasive that virtually every action can be regarded as giving rise to externalities of some form. There are three kinds of distinction which may possibly be used in determining the applicability of the concept. One would be to

[6]*Higher Education,* Report of the Committee on Higher Education, H.M.S.O., London 1963, par. 625.

distinguish real from psychic effects, a second would be to separate distributional from other changes, and a third would be to focus on marginal rather than non-marginal effects.

The distinction between 'real' and 'psychic' effects may be illustrated by the introduction of additional motor-cars on to a road system, creating 'externalities' for the original set of motorists, in this case of a negative rather than a positive kind. These costs may be of a 'psychic' nature in that the additional vehicles lessen one's chances of enjoying an open stretch of road, or extra vehicles may make some drivers anxious and nervous, or the noise created by passing vehicles may become an irritant. Some of the costs may also be real in that extra vehicles may slow down traffic flow, leading to increased braking and associated adjustments in speed, or they may create bottlenecks and lengthen journey time, or they may raise the probability of accidents, all of which would result in increased operating costs for motoring. While it may become difficult to distinguish the two, in some instances the classification into 'real' and 'psychic' effects can be helpful in tackling the question of valuing externalities. For rate-of-return calculations, it is the real effects (those which give rise to monetary consequences) which are relevant.

The second distinction, that between distributional and other externalities, is more difficult to define satisfactorily and almost certainly more difficult to treat in practice, but nevertheless can be helpful in clarifying some aspects. An illustration might be Weisbrod's example, quoted in the previous chapter, of the benefits which an individual derived from education in being enabled to fill up his own tax returns. Against this, however, there would be a loss to some tax accountant who would experience a reduced demand for his services. In this case, the gain and loss may be taken as cancelling each other out, so that the increase or decrease in community output is zero, the net effect being a redistribution of income from accountants to the educated. Once the size of the group involved becomes significant, however, the task of distinguishing these distributional changes becomes more complex. If a large group of taxpayers, for example, switch from accountants to self-completion, the fall in demand for the former's services would lead to a reduction in their numbers. Similarly the time allocated by the taxpayers to self-completion may be expected to have some opportunity cost in terms of alternative output forgone by them.

This problem of the potential price and quantity movements associated with group effects leads to the third distinction, that between marginal and non-marginal changes. Some of the illustrations of the externalities created by education refer to effects which are so diffused throughout the economy that the whole basis for their valuation becomes dubious. If it is suggested that the education of some groups raises the productivity of other workers, so that the former's earnings do not fully reflect their contribution to output, this indicates that their withdrawal will lead to a fall in output greater than their salaries. Any estimate of the probable fall in output which would be associated with, say, the withdrawal of all graduates from the labour force would immediately face the problem that the alternative structure of output would be characterised both by significantly different quantities and relative prices for various items; and this would remove the basis for direct comparison between the two positions. The normal approach of comparing the two situations, that with and that without the item in question, can then only be directly applied to marginal situations, where the change is so small that secondary repercussions throughout the economy may safely be ignored. The practical question is to decide the point at which calculations grounded on the marginal hypothesis became dangerously suspect. No specific answer to this problem exists; it is always necessary therefore to query in each specific case whether the size of the effects warrants the application of marginalist calculations.

The various external benefits suggested by Weisbrod can to some extent be related to each of these three aspects. The child-care service provided by schools which in turn benefits mothers may be considered as giving rise to a real benefit, if its presence enables mothers, who otherwise would not do so, to work, or if its absence would result in the hiring of alternative forms of child-care. If attendance at school is voluntary, this latter aspect could be possibly of some importance, since the decision to send the child to school would have taken into account the costs of alternative arrangements for child-care (and education). In such cases child-care need not be an external benefit associated with schooling, since schooling would be bought as a joint-product offering both educational and child-care services. It would only be if school attendance for the child was compulsory that the child-care service could be unambiguously viewed as an external by-product for the mother. It may be observed, however, that in cases where it produces the 'psychic' benefit of increased leisure-time, the benefit need not always be positive: some mothers may experience a loss of satisfaction from the absence of their child.

Finally there is the question whether valuing this benefit for those working mothers who otherwise might not have been employed in terms of their earnings is valid, since the withdrawal of all such mothers might constitute a non-marginal change.

Apart from problems of classification, however, the more continuing difficulty with external effects is to establish their relative magnitude, or indeed even the direction which they take, that is, whether they constitute costs or benefits to others. Effects on neighbours can serve as a case in point. Weisbrod, in common with many other writers, suggests that education may result in lower crime rates. West, who shows the long history which this proposition enjoys, suggests that the available data do not support it, and if anything, would point to a contrary conclusion.[7] Crime rates for young people in post-war Britain appear from the available data to have risen rather than fallen, despite the expansion in education during the period. Moreover, there is some evidence that the last year of compulsory education was the heaviest one for juvenile delinquency, and that the tendency towards crime during school years was reversed when pupils left school and went to work. Thus, one effect of raising the school-leaving age from 14 to 15 in 1947, was that 'there was an immediate change over in the delinquency record of the 13-year-olds (who until this had been the most troublesome age-group) and the 14-year-olds, who

[7]E. G. West, *Education and the State*, Institute of Economic Affairs, London 1965.
D

took their place in 1948, and have held it consistently ever since'.[8]

The apparent negative effect in these cases may be associated with the fact that the education in question was compulsory, and the young people concerned had no desire of their own to attend school. It might still be the case for older age-groups, then, that the external effects on neighbours would be positive. Vaizey refers to the students' wilful desires to do good to others for nothing as an example, which would certainly suggest a positive externality. Equally, there are cases where these 'wilful desires' might not be interpreted as beneficial. The student riots, which have been a feature of contemporary life in many European and American countries, may, for example, be regarded as 'good' or 'criminal' by different sectors of the population.

While it may be agreed then, that the available evidence undoubtedly supports the view that education affects neighbours, it is a different question to decide the direction or value of such effects. Indeed, these effects may well constitute a non-marginal case, in that any valuation may be affected by the value-judgements of the individual making them.

Less striking illustrations of the same problem are furnished by some of the other examples given. It is not clear, for example, how such things as voluntary community activities, choral groups, drama clubs, local art shows etc. might be counted as benefits. Many of them would appear to be activities which are largely confined, both as regards participants and spectators, to educated people and represent a form of consumption activity for them. It could be argued that education confers a benefit by extending the individual's range of consumption activities, but this is not necessarily so. As one writer puts it, 'the graduated student now gets psychic return from having been educated to appreciate Bach, but he can no longer tolerate the Beatles'.[9] Hence, in many instances education may substitute one range of consumption possibilities for another. It would be a specific

---

[8] *Ibid.*, 36, quoting Crowther Report, London 1959.
[9] J. Wiseman, 'Cost Benefit Analysis in Education', *Southern Economic Journal*, July 1965.

value-judgement to say that one set constituted an improvement and hence conferred a benefit, though it is the sort of value-judgement which many would be prepared to make. The other side of the coin should also be noted. The tastes of educated people tend to be more expensive in many respects when compared with those of less educated people. To discuss these matters fully would take us too far from the point at issue, which is the valuation of neighbourhood effects of education. The more immediate problem of identifying or measuring long-run 'neighbour' effects does not appear to be tractable at the overall level. Thus, if any one activity is considered, such as amateur dramatics, then the addition of each new potential actor, through his education, may be thought of as creating benefits (or disbenefits) for the existing group, depending on its size. In the early stages when numbers are small, the benefits might be positive, in that a minimum number of interested people will be needed before plays can be performed, and each additional member adds to the scope of activities. Thereafter, the effect is less certain and disbenefits may be created for those who are displaced by newcomers. Though there may be positive benefits for the remainder of the cast, the overall effect is thus uncertain. If numbers of potential actors continue to rise, a second drama group may be formed, resulting in a positive benefit. All that can be said by way of generalisation is that effects on neighbours are undoubtedly created, but their magnitude and even direction is not clear in any one instance.

Some of the employment-related benefits raise similar problems. The effect which the introduction of educated personnel may have on the productivity of other members in a group is, for example, something which in principle is measure-able, because the earnings of the latter would be higher after the appearance on the scene of the educated personnel. But this assumes that earnings would accurately reflect productivity. It would not suffice that the approximate relationship between the two should be approximately correct, because presumably (though this is a complete assumption) the external effect would in most cases make only marginal contributions to the output of the members concerned. In practice, earnings are unlikely to react so precisely to productivity changes. More-over, the position can be further complicated because intro-ducing different types of personnel may be associated with changes in equipment or production methods, so that the portion of any increase attributable to the personnel could be indeterminate.

Even looser links might be expected in the chain which would run from increased education via new knowledge and invention to the raising of output and income in the economy. This proposition which again recurs frequently, is not of course an externality of education as such. The notion is rather that education forms a necessary joint input along with research, in the expansion of the output potential of an economy, and that the returns to these activities, whether considered jointly or separately, understate their overall contribution. No attempt will be made to examine this problem here since changes in products and techniques of production do not appear to be amenable to treatment in terms of externalities. It is simpler to state the problem, and accept that with existing knowledge it is not possible to incorporate any calculation for these effects in social rates-of-return.

The relevance of these processes to an examination of economic growth is a topic which will be treated separately in chapter five.

Even in this case of education being a joint input to the growth process, it should be noted that its effects are not always unambiguously of a positive character. It is frequently asserted, for example, that schools and colleges are a con-servative element, and far from promoting growth, may hinder it by their emphasis on traditional behaviour patterns. A separate, but closely related suggestion is that whether con-servative or radical, the educational ethos can be inimical to growth because it accords to business and economic activities a much lower status than to 'cultural', 'academic', 'intellectual', 'artistic' or similar attributes. Again then, there is probably universal agreement that education has definite impacts on the economy's growth and development; the disputable issue is whether on balance it does so in a positive or negative manner.

IV

In contrast to the extended qualitative discussions of the social value of education, quantitative estimates are sparse. As Becker remarks, when introducing his own brief treatment of this aspect, 'economists (and others) have generally had little success in estimating the social effects of different investments, and, unfortunately education is no exception.'[10]

On the returns side, the social gain was taken by Becker as being the direct taxes paid by individuals from the additional income associated with education. One of the statistical problems here is to select an appropriate tax rate to apply to lifetime earnings; if income-tax rates rise over time, the use of the base-year would overstate the private, and understate the social, portion of the gross earnings concerned. Thus for the U.S., Becker indicates that income tax accounted for only 1·5 per cent of 1939 incomes but for 7·5 and 10 per cent of 1949 and 1956 incomes. These changes are a product both of rising incomes, which can bring the individual into a higher tax bracket within a given tax structure, and of increased tax rates, which raise the proportion payable in tax from any given income. Both elements were catered for in a relatively crude way by Becker since a more sophisticated adjustment would not have much effect on the results.

Direct social costs of education were estimated by first obtaining the total current spending of the institutions concerned (high schools and colleges), and then deducting from this expenditure on research and other non-educational items. An estimate was next made of the appropriate fraction of capital costs which should be attributed to each year. Indirect social costs were measured in terms of the gross earnings forgone by students. Of the total social costs (direct and indirect) the student paid about three-quarters, though their share of the direct costs, as measured by fees, was only about one-third. Indirect costs then accounted for about three-fifths and direct, two-fifths, of total costs.

[10]Becker, *Human Capital*, New York 1964, 117.

In the case of college education, the social rates-of-return which emerge from this data, without making any adjustment for ability, are 13 per cent for the 1939 and over 12 per cent for the 1949 urban male white graduates. These are slightly lower than the comparable estimates of private returns, which it will be recalled were 14·5 and 13 per cent respectively. A similar pattern, with the social below the private rate, was found for the other categories of student. Becker feels that the estimates may be treated as indicating the lower limit to the correct social rate-of-return. The development of more refined estimates was not considered to be feasible but he refers to some estimates of Denison (which will be discussed in chapter five) that may serve as a guide to the upper limit. These yield an estimate of the growth in knowledge, which, if allocated to education on the same proportionate basis as earnings, would result in a social rate-of-return on college education of 25 per cent.

Social rates-of-return calculated on a similar basis to Becker's were also presented for the two U.K. studies discussed in chapter three.[11] In the first of these, the social rates-of-return for three years upper secondary school and the six years for this, plus university education, were 12 per cent and 8 per cent respectively. The comparable private rates had been estimated at 10 and 14 per cent. In the second inter-firm study, the social rates-of-return on average showed a closer correspondence to private rates. Thus, for each of the six higher educational levels considered the social rates-of-return, considering the base level, were on average $7\frac{1}{2}$, $10\frac{1}{2}$, 9, $9\frac{1}{2}$, 8 and 10 per cent, while the corresponding private rates were 7, 10, 10, $11\frac{1}{4}$, $10\frac{1}{2}$ and $11\frac{1}{2}$ per cent respectively.

Weisbrod has presented estimates of some of the external benefits discussed by him. In the case of 'residence-related' benefits, he gives a figure of $2,000 million as the possible annual value of the child-care service provided for working mothers who have young children at school. This benefit is treated as a return on primary education, a level which has not been discussed in rate-of-return terms here, but some

[11]Blaug, *op. cit.*; Blaug, Peston and Ziderman, *The Utilisation of Educated Manpower in Industry*, Edinburgh 1967.

indication of the relative impact of this figure would be to set it alongside the estimated annual cost of $8,000 million for primary education.

A second residence-related benefit, which future children would derive from the present-day education of their parents, is valued in a later study.[12] Using data on the additional education which children of more educated parents receive, the value in higher earnings of this extra education of the child is estimated. These expected higher earnings of the child are then expressed as a rate-of-return to the parent's education. Calculations are made for five different educational levels, and two separate cohorts, using three different cost estimates and two discount rates. This gives a total of 60 possible cases; for 42 of these the results show that the potential return to the child was sufficient to cover the whole cost of the parents' education, and still yield some positive rate-of-return (ranging from $\frac{1}{4}$ to 8 per cent). In 14 of the remaining cases the expected effect was sufficient to cover varying portions of the cost, leaving only 4 cases of the 60 in which the effect was negligible. These estimates are to be treated cautiously as the authors emphasise, since they were of necessity based on a set of assumptions, not all of which would apply in practice to many cases, but they are nevertheless of interest in illustrating again the substantial size which some of these educational externalities may assume in practice.

Finally, in this section on empirical studies it may be useful to refer to another Weisbrod study on a somewhat separate aspect of education.[13] This was an analysis of programmes operated in the St Louis area to prevent young people dropping out from high school. For the samples studied the results showed that although the subsequent earnings of those who stayed on were more than sufficient to cover the additional teaching costs involved, they were considerably below the cost of the special measures designed to retain them in school. Thus, from the social viewpoint it was not an economic proposition to

[12]B. Weisbrod and W. Swift, 'On the Monetary Value of Education's Inter-generation Effects', *Journal of Political Economy*, December 1965.

[13] B. Weisbrod, 'Preventing High School Dropouts', in *Measuring Benefits of Government Investments*, Washington 1965, 117–149.

operate the remedial programme. The usual caveats apply however to straightforward interpretations of this kind; in particular it should be observed that no estimate was available of benefits external to the student which might result from preventing a drop out.

V

The theoretical and practical problems which arise in attempting to assess the economic value of education in cost/benefit terms have now been touched upon. It has been seen that apart from the range of difficulties which occur when evaluating education from an individual viewpoint, broadening the basis of assessment to include effects in the rest of the community concerned added yet further complexities.

Perhaps the least controversial aspect, and also the one which clearly shows the relevance of social calculations, are 'social' rates-of-return of the Becker/Blaug type. Since individuals do not bear the full cost of their education, nor capture the complete increment in their earning power, it is clearly relevant to know the effect on calculated rates-of-return made by the use of total cost and total benefit valuation.

The rather narrow concept of total cost/benefit used, and the limited interpretative value which these 'social' calculations possess, should, however, be emphasised. While the cost reductions which students receive and the subsequent income-tax payments which they make are undoubtedly two important examples of the species, they by no means exhaust the possible range of 'externalities' which arise from education. One reason for using these items as the basis for 'social' calculations is that they refer to public-sector transactions. As such, they represent a clear-cut distinction between individual financial transactions, on the one hand, and real resource effects on the other.

In contrast, it was seen that many other types of possible externality gave rise to various complications. Some, for example, might represent money transfers between individuals which, while they would affect the distribution of income, would not lead to any net change in output. This does not imply that distributional aspects are unimportant, but rather that they are completely distinct (at least conceptually) from the allocative questions of resource use and valuation.

On this distributional aspect it is worth digressing to note that the differences between the private and social rate-of-return are not to be taken as providing a comprehensive assessment of the way in which the benefits are distributed between the individual and other groups. The higher incomes educated people receive will also mean a higher level of consumption spending on their part than would otherwise have been possible. Any indirect taxes levied on this greater spending will also mean increased tax revenues and this should be counted. It would doubtless be necessary to standardise expenditure patterns by educational level in order to make such calculations accurately, but this obstacle should not prove to be insurmountable. In addition to knowing how the total tax payments of people change as a result of education, it would also be necessary to ascertain how receipts of public sector services, for which the full cost is not levied, are affected. If, for example, these were to fall as a result of less unemployment, or of less need for subsidised services such as housing or health, then there is again a gain to the rest of the community. Data on the distribution of public services by income and education would again help in estimating these effects. The actual redistribution of income, which results from education, is then something which will differ substantially from that implied by social rates-of-return.

Reverting to our main theme, it was seen that attempts to measure the externalities associated with education give rise to formidable problems. Despite the ingenious attempts to measure some of these, such as Weisbrod's illustrations of the child-care aspect of education to mothers, benefits to future children, or the services which educated people provide for themselves, the feeling remains that these are but a scratch on the surface of this question. Benefits to the community at large in particular pose a major problem. What is the precise nature of these benefits and how important are they? Wiseman, in referring to these, is critical of the vague illustrations which are frequently used—'cultural advance, providing an informed electorate', 'improving the qualities of leadership' and so forth. He questions first whether these are economic benefits at all, and if so, who is competent to value them, and secondly whether they are not rather a reflection of the wider social values of society. The probability is that they are both. A well-informed electorate may constitute one of the non-economic goals of society, but it also is in some ways a technical necessity for the efficient functioning of a modern economy. The nature and degree of the information which would go to make an electorate 'informed', would again reflect value judgements as to the rightness of the system envisaged. Eastern economists are technically capable of operating a pricing system if they wish, just as western ones can apply planning techniques. Their choices are influenced by judgements which combine economic and non-economic elements. Likewise the effects of the systems are evaluated by techniques whose acceptance requires a certain type of value judgement. In a sense, it is meaningless to ask, for example, whether the inculcation of an acceptance of law is an economic benefit to a western economy, for without some acceptance of it, a market economy is totally impracticable.

These difficulties are mainly the consequence of setting tasks which marginalist economic theory is not capable of tackling. The need to adhere to marginal calculations as distinct from total or average measurements had already emerged when considering the private rate-of-return approach. This need is much greater in the social case. The cost-benefit approach is not designed and was never intended to tackle such questions as the contribution of education to reducing crime or making democracy effective. What may be feasible is to assess the effect which marginal changes in education may have. Will, for example, raising the number of graduates by a small percentage lead to positive, negative or any desirable external effects of this kind, or reducing slightly the numbers who drop out at the end of compulsory schooling? Changes such as these which can be fitted into the marginal framework of other things remaining equal, are the ones which hold out the prospect for fruitful future development. The Weisbrod study of school drop-outs in one area is a most interesting and valuable prototype of this approach for despite its inability to present measures for many of the items, the problem was at least being formulated in a more appropriate manner.

One further issue avoided in the discussion relates to those effects which are not captured in rate-of-return measures; namely the direct consumption or psychic effects noted earlier. These effects, it was seen, may be either positive or negative in value, and this further obscures the interpretation of rate-of-return data. Thus, if one wishes to contend that the consumer always maximises his satisfaction, the presence of higher returns on education as compared with other forms of investment can be taken as indicating that these psychic effects have a negative value equivalent to this observed difference in returns. On the other hand, the existence of these differences in returns may be used either to infer the presence of a disequilibrium or of 'irrational' choices.

A somewhat different problem arises with these effects at the social level. It was observed that one such effect of education might be not only to add to the range of consumption possibilities open to the individual, but also to change them. This could mean that the *ex-post* or realised value of psychic effects may differ from their *ex-ante* or expected value. Blaug (rightly) argues that it is the latter valuation which is relevant to the individual when taking his decision. At the social level, however, it is *ex-post* values which are the more likely relevant ones since the framework within which social policies are formulated and implemented is shaped by observed behaviour. In taking decisions on educational matters, the relevant social consideration might not be the expectations of individuals regarding their future behaviour, but rather the expectations of the decision makers regarding the actual behaviour of people. If it were known, for example, that certain courses had the effect of producing a more law-abiding or politically responsible community, policy makers might introduce them even though none of the individuals concerned might be conscious of, or expect, this result. Hence the possibility of a divergence between the private and social valuations of psychic effects may arise.

The dangers inherent in such divergences of views are well known; at one extreme they may lead to the view that the individual does not know what is good for him, whereas the state does. The other extreme of accepting individual choice as sacrosanct is likewise to evade the problem, since there is a difference in kind and not merely of degree between the choices of the two groups. The difficulties of attempting to cope with such problems have been discussed by Wiseman, who, *inter alia*, rejects the suggestion that educational policy decisions be reserved to the educated on the grounds that they understand the value of education better than the uneducated.[14] The problem here is to decide who is competent to assess the 'correct' value, or to adjudicate on conflicting values, of education and it is one which has not yet been satisfactorily resolved in any society. In practice the working compromise to be found in most societies is that which is effected through the political process. As such, it is no longer a problem within the economic sphere. One way, however, in which some useful economic data on the magnitude of these effects might still be obtained would be to ask for estimates of the value placed on these consumption benefits by various groups, both before and after they had been educated. In this way some indication, however crude, of the relative importance of these benefits might be obtained.

It is not, however, the intention to speculate here on the possible forms which future development of the cost-benefit approach might take. The present chapter has been concerned with the somewhat different question of the nature and techniques for making a community-wide appraisal of education in economic terms. It was seen that while the rate-of-return approach can be usefully applied to this question, the problems associated with it are such that it is unlikely, in itself, to provide an adequate perspective on the economic role which education plays in the modern economy.

[14]Wiseman, *art. cit.*

CHAPTER 5

EDUCATION AND ECONOMIC GROWTH

THE approach adopted in the previous chapters in which education was treated as a type of investment, while providing many valuable insights into the problem, does not provide a comprehensive picture of the economic relevance of education. In this chapter a somewhat different aspect will be explored, namely, the role which education may play in the process of economic growth.

Growth has come to the forefront in the range of economic policy objectives during the post-war period. There are several influences both economic and non-economic which appear to have converged in order to produce this emphasis on growth. One was an increased awareness of the extreme poverty which characterised so much of the world's population, giving rise to the desire for policies to remedy this position. A second was the emergence of the Soviet Union as a world power, which focussed attention on the growth performance of western economies, not only in terms of whether planning or competition gave the 'best' results, but also on the need, for security reasons, to expand output at a rate fast enough to sustain the requirements of a growing military sector.

Coupled with these motives was the improved understanding of the workings and limitations of the market-type economy. So long as the perfectly competitive model was accepted as being relevant for policy purposes, then there was no apparent scope for any separate measures aimed at such questions as growth, because these would have been accommodated within the structure. Growth, i.e. the raising of future output, would require either some addition to productive resources or some more effective method of utilising given resources. Of the three categories of available resources, land was fixed in quantity, while if the growth objective was defined more precisely as raising output (income) per head, then an increase in the quantity of labour would not help. This would leave the third category, capital, as the resource whose quantity could be increased. To bring about such an increase, and also to discover some more effective methods of using given resources, would call for the diversion of current resources away from consumption into investment. In other words, growth entailed a choice between consumption now, and consumption in the future. These choices would be made by the usual process of comparing the expected return on the investment with the opportunity cost (a process which has been illustrated in chapter three). This would apply not only to cases where, in large-scale business investment, the savings and investment decisions might be taken by separate groups, but also where they are inseparably linked as a complete individual decision, such as the traditional Robinson Crusoe example of abstaining from fishing today (and therefore consumption today), in order to make a net for more effective fishing tomorrow. In each case, choices which will raise future output are seen as entailing comparisons between the consumer's time-preference for present versus future goods, and the productivity of the investment in raising the flow of future output.

With the competitive model, if each individual makes his preferred allocations between present and future positions, he is in effect choosing the growth path for his own lifetime consumption; and what is true for one will, by aggregating individual data, be also true for the economy.

The economic challenge to this competitive determination of an economy's growth rate came in two ways, one practical, the second theoretical. The practical objection was based on the experiences of the 1920s and 1930s when large scale unemployment could no longer be regarded as a purely temporary phenomenon associated with adjusting from one equilibrium position to another. Instead, there was an increasing tendency to regard it as something which was endemic to a 'mature' or wealthy economy. A main theme of Keynes' general theory was the suggestion that it is possible for an economy to have persisting 'involuntary' unemployment because of an inadequate level of aggregate demand. While Keynesian economics is primarily concerned with the short-run question of generating full employment in any given period, the treatment of the problem clearly has long-run implications because the growth record of an economy which experiences persistent chronic unemployment is likely to differ from that of another enjoying full employment.

The theoretical questioning of the competitive model also grew out of the 'externalities' aspect discussed in chapter four. If it really was the case that not all of the benefits or costs associated with an activity might accrue to the individual(s) concerned, then their evaluations and decisions would be based on only partial data. Social calculations would yield different results, and a different allocation between present and future goods. Left in this general form, it is possible that social evaluation could call for either greater or smaller allocations to future consumption. However, since Pigou suggested 'people distributed their resources between the present, the near future and the remote future on the basis of a wholly irrational preference', because their 'telescopic' faculty is defective, there has been a widespread recognition that private rates of time-preference may be higher than their social counterpart.[1] Apart from any 'defective assessment' of future satisfaction, a second reason why private time-preference rates may be higher, is because the future is more uncertain for the individual than for the community.

But while it may be interesting to know that social rates of time-preference are below private rates, the concept cannot be very useful unless there is some way of estimating the extent of the difference. Since it is not known whether social rates-of-return on investment are greater, or less, than private rates, there is no direct inference to be made concerning the 'correct' allocation as between present and future goods.

In combination, however, the heightened awareness of 'externalities', together with the development of Keynesian 'disequilibrium' economics, added substantial economic weight to the non-economic pressures which were causing govern-

---

[1] A. C. Pigou, *Economics of Welfare*, fourth edition, London 1932, 25.

ments to take a specific interest in the question of economic growth. Out of this interest has grown the myriad of programmes and policy measures of the past two decades.

Associated with this, there has been a continual interest by economists in analysing the nature and causes of economic growth. Much of the initial work grew out of Keynesian economics and was concerned with extending the analysis to take account of the effects on aggregate supply. The emphasis in Keynes' work had been on identifying the level of demand needed to generate or sustain full employment, and with explaining fluctuations in the level of demand. Investment emerged as the volatile demand element; consequently many of the initial policy prescriptions were concerned with influencing the volume of investment, raising it when unemployment existed and curbing it if inflation or excessive demand pressures existed. This demand-oriented analysis, despite its value, did not, however, take account of the longer-run supply effect which investment has in raising the capacity to produce. The extensions necessary to incorporate these supply effects grew rapidly, following on the pioneering work of Harrod[2] and Domar.[3] By emphasising the link between capital and output, this approach, though not in itself designed as an explanation of the growth process, provided a useful basis for the development of such theories. In its growth form, the theory focusses on the ratio which must be maintained through time, between the capital stock and the level of output. Whether this ratio is something which is fixed by technological factors, or whether it is susceptible to influence by other elements in the system is something which was less clear.

II

Apart from attempts at theoretical refinement, various statistical estimates aimed at establishing the impact of investment on growth rates have been undertaken, in recent years. The

[2]R. Harrod, 'An Essay in Dynamic Theory', *Economic Journal*, 1939.
[3]E. Domar, 'Capital Expansion, Rate of Growth and Employment', *Econometrica*, 1946.

general outcome of these has been to show that while investment undoubtedly played an important part, it was by no
means as dominant an element as many economists had earlier
thought. A typical illustration of these statistical results is
given by the following data.

Estimated Contribution of Inputs to Growth in Output: Selected Countries.
Annual Averages (%)

Countries	(a) Contribution of Labour and Capital		(b) 'Residual'	
	ECE 1949/59	NIESR 1950/60	ECE	NIESR
Germany	2·9	3·75	4·5	4·05
France	1·1	1·45	3·4	2·95
Norway	1·6	2·05	1·8	1·15
U.S.A.		1·9		1·2
U.K.	1·3	1·15	1·1	1·2

Source: *The British Economy in 1975* (Ed. W. Beckerman), National
Institute for Economic and Social Research, London 1964.

The interpretation of these data is that of the estimated
annual growth in output of 7·8 per cent for Germany in the
1950s, increases in the amounts of capital and labour can be
used to account for a 3·75 per cent increase, leaving the remaining four per cent unexplained. This residual is the
increased 'productivity' per unit of input employed, and it
may be noted that the absolute size of this residual is greater,
the larger the growth rate concerned.

While the size of the 'residual' element may have been a
surprise, the existence of some long-run influences, other than
quantity changes in labour and capital, had long been recognised. The most obvious of these was 'technological progress'
(which through the introduction of new production techniques

and new products would raise the output of any given factors). The determinants of such progress were in turn taken to be the products of invention and innovation. Traditionally, the tendency had been to regard inventions as something which were the fruits of creative genius and consequently in large part beyond the control or influence of economic factors. Innovation, the process of harnessing new inventions and exploiting them for commercial purposes, depended on the actions of business entrepreneurs, who could always be expected to avail of any new opportunities for profit. The growth of modern large scale research on an organised basis has produced a shift in this emphasis; it is now seen as an industry which, despite its greater uncertainties and other special elements, can be regarded as amenable to economic evaluation and influence.

It was quickly recognised that research and development (R+D) activities, as they are now described, had many links with education. While applied research with commercial orientations might be mainly the concern of business organisations, much of the basic or fundamental research on which it was based was the product of universities, and related institutions. Apart from this direct role of providing a flow of research results, universities were also of relevance as the suppliers of the highly-skilled personnel needed for R+D activities.

While it is undoubtedly a factor of relevance, the role of R+D in generating growth is one which still remains unclear. There does not appear to be any direct link, for example, between a country's level of spending on R+D and its growth rate, since countries which spend relatively large proportions of their national income in this way, such as the U.S. and U.K., have had lower growth rates than others with smaller spending, such as Japan, Germany or France. While there are many factors which can be, and have been, advanced to account for differential effects of this type, such as the proportion of defence activities, or the extent to which 'know-how' is bought from abroad, no comprehensive assessment of the link between R+D and growth is yet available.

If it is taken that the effect of technological progress is primarily to produce a change in the quality of the capital inputs employed, a logical extension would be to apply the same notion to labour, and to investigate the extent to which changes in the quality, as distinct from the quantity, of labour had taken place. This development of human resources could be the product of many things, such as improved health, better nutrition and living conditions, more training on the job—and also more education. It was seen in the two previous chapters that the rewards could in many cases be sufficient to induce people to invest in their own capital development rather than in the development of some piece of physical equipment.

The potential importance of human resource development can be illustrated by some estimates which Schultz has made of the amount of capital formation represented by education.[4] These show that over the period 1900 to 1957, the stock of education for people in the labour force as measured by the costs of producing it, has risen from an estimated \$63 billion in 1900 to \$535 billion in 1957, both series measured in terms of 1956 schooling costs. These stocks were equivalent to 22 per cent and 42 per cent respectively of physical assets (or more accurately of non-human reproducible wealth) in the same years. In absolute terms, educational capital could clearly be a significant element in production, and what is perhaps more interesting, if it had risen at a faster rate over the period was becoming relatively more important. Over the period the stock of education in the labour force rose by $8\frac{1}{2}$ times, whereas the rise in reproducible non-human wealth was $4\frac{1}{2}$ times. While there are many problems which surround attempts to measure the capital formation represented by education and which consequently demand that estimates such as Schultz's be interpreted with care, the concept is clearly one of relevance to an analysis of the growth process.[5]

The more important step, however, is to explore the feasibility of measuring the contribution which changes in the quality of the labour force may have on the level of output.

[4]T. W. Schultz, 'Rise in the Capital Stock represented by Education in the U.S., 1900–57', in *Economics of Higher Education*, ed. S. Mushkin, Washington 1962.
[5]M. J. Bowman, 'Human Capital: Concepts and Measures', in *Economics of Higher Education, op. cit.*

nost comprehensive treatment to date of this aspect is
of Denison, who has made detailed estimates of the
ive contribution which both quality and quantity changes
... he various elements have had on the role of growth in output.

Denison's first study dealt with the U.S. over the period
1909 to 1957.[6] In all, twenty factors of either a quantity or
quality nature which might affect output were examined.
The total period was divided into two sections, 1909–29 and
1929–57. The growth rate in real national income was an
estimated 2·82 per cent per annum in the first period and
2·93 per cent in the second. Of these totals, additions to the
capital stock were estimated to have accounted for ·73 per
cent and ·43 per cent respectively. Changes in the labour
force contributed an estimated 1·53 per cent and 1·57 per
cent respectively, made up of both quantity and quality
components. The major quantity changes were increases in
the total numbers employed, and decreases in the length of
the working week. The major quality change was education,
which contributed an estimated ·35 per cent and ·67 per cent
respectively to the totals in each period.

In total, then, changes in capital and labour inputs accounted for 2·26 per cent and 2·0 per cent respectively, leaving
the residual productivity increases at ·56 per cent and ·93 per
cent. For the second period, the residual was allocated over a
range of other factors; the two most important of which were
advances in knowledge, which accounted for ·58 per cent, and
economies of scale, accounting for ·35 per cent.

On the basis of these estimates, education would thus
appear to have been a significant source of economic growth,
accounting for an apparent 12 per cent of total growth in the
first, and for 23 per cent in the second period. If advances in
knowledge are also taken as having educational implications,
the relative importance of education is further enhanced.

A later study by Denison which dealt with the U.S. and
western Europe over the period 1950/1962, presents a rather

[6]E. Denison, *The Sources of Economic Growth in the United States*, Paper No. 13,
Committee for Economic Development, New York 1962.

strong contrast to the initial one.[7] In only three of the nine countries studied did education account for more than 10 per cent of the total growth rate. These were the U.S. with 15 per cent, and Belgium and the U.K. each with 13 per cent. Of the remaining six, Norway and Italy yielded estimates of 7 per cent, France 6 per cent, Netherlands 5 per cent, Denmark 4 per cent and Germany 2 per cent. In the European countries, factors such as economies of scale and structural changes—especially the shift from agriculture to other forms of employment—were of greater relative importance than had been the case in the U.S. Advances in knowledge were estimated to have contributed a ·76 per cent growth rate in each of the countries during the period. Given the differences in the overall growth rates this meant that its relative importance varied from a contribution of 11 per cent to the German growth rate of 7·26 per cent, to a 33 per cent share of the U.K. figure of 2·29 per cent.

III

The degree of acceptance accorded to these estimates will be influenced by attitudes towards the validity of the measurement procedures adopted. Denison's calculations are based on the distribution of income among the various factors of production in each year. His basic assumption is that income received is a measure of the contribution which each particular factor makes to output. In other words the estimates are based on a marginal productivity theory of income distribution. Since this is not accepted as valid by all economists, it is important to be aware both of the main characteristics of the theory and of the objections which have been raised against it.

First the theory assumes the existence of competitive industries. This will imply that each factor unit of comparable quality will receive the same payments—workers of comparable skill etc. will be paid the same wage rate. A second

[7] E. Denison, *Why Growth Rates Differ: Postwar Experience in Nine Western Countries*, Washington 1967.

assumption is that firms seek to maximise profits; to achieve this they will employ any factor up to the point at which the value of output contributed by the last unit employed will just equal the payments which must be made to it. In combination these two assumptions will also imply that the average and marginal payment made to any factor will be identical. Thirdly, there is an assumption that the proportions in which factors are combined to product output can be altered, which means that substitution can take place as between factors. This would enable the contribution which any one factor makes to output to be evaluated. Fourthly, it is assumed that the sum of the marginal products of each factor equals total product. This implies that there are what is termed constant returns to scale in output, meaning, for example, that a 1 per cent increase in the quantity of each factor employed would produce a 1 per cent increase in output. Similarly, for a small increase in any one factor, the change in output which would result could be inferred from the share of total income enjoyed by that factor. Thus, if labour accounts for 70 per cent of total income, then a 1 per cent rise in labour, with capital and other inputs remaining constant, could be expected to yield an 0.7 per cent increase in output. Calculations of this latter form, for changes in one input, would only be valid for small increases, since any substantial rise could be expected to result in diminishing returns setting in. Finally, it may be noted that marginal productivity measurements assume the absence of 'externalities' which would cause a divergence between the private and social value of a factor.

In the particular case of education, Denison based his estimates on data relating to the differential earnings associated with the educational levels of individuals, and on the amount of education people in the labour force possessed at different dates. The first of these factors need not be examined here, since the relationship between earnings and education has been already extensively discussed in chapter three. It is worth noting, however, that again not all of the higher earnings of the educated were attributed to their education; in this instance Denison allocated 60 per cent to this cause, leaving 40 per cent as the adjustment for other influences such as ability. Denison describes this three-fifths assumption as 'one of three major assumptions in this study that importantly affect the results at which I shall ultimately arrive for the sources of past growth, and that do not flow arithmetically from any data that can be adduced'.[8] In a subsequent paper dealing with the same topic, Denison introduced, as evidence in support of his assumption, one of the studies which Becker had used when making his adjustment for the influence of ability.[9] This study yielded results very close to Denison's assumptions, and suggested that if anything, the latter had somewhat underestimated the contribution of education to the total earnings differential.

In order to assess the contribution to growth, the second factor to be considered was changes in the amounts of education. In addition to taking account of the increase which took place in the average number of years' education acquired by members of the labour force over the period, Denison also allowed for the increase which had occurred in the numbers of days attended at school in each year. His calculations for the rise in the average amount of education possessed by people in the labour force are thus based on the rise in the total number of days attended at school. In the decade 1940–50, for example, there was a rise of 10·4 per cent in the average number of years schooling completed, and also a 10·9 per cent rise in the average number of days attended per school year; the combined effect of these two factors was a significant rise of 22·4 per cent in the total number of days at school. Denison, in the second study referred to, notes that his estimates are very similar to those obtained by Schultz (in the study quoted above) for 'equivalent years of schooling', at different dates.

The procedure for calculating the effect which this extra schooling will have on earnings was as follows. The base year to which data on earnings differentials related was 1949. Taking three-fifths as the fraction of these attributable to

[8]*Ibid.*, 67–70.

[9]E. Denison, 'Measuring the Contribution of Education to Economic Growth', in *The Residual Factor and Economic Growth*, O.E.C.D., Paris 1964.

education, the relative earnings of people with varying education could then be expressed in percentage terms. For example, taking 8 years as 100, 12 years equalled 124, 13 to 15 as 139 and so forth, the interpretation being that a person with 12 years schooling could on average earn 24 per cent more than one with 8 years. Using this 1949 scale the effect of additional education on earnings could then be calculated. For the 22·4 per cent increase in schooling in the 1940s, the calculated rise in earnings was 9·9 per cent. This means that an increase of almost 1 per cent per annum in earnings was attributed to education for this decade.

The other component of most relevance to education, the 'advances in knowledge', does not call for any elaboration. The 19 factors directly analysed having accounted for 80 per cent of the 1929-1957 observed growth, the remaining 20 per cent was then attributed to advances in knowledge.

A comprehensive discussion of both the theoretical and practical aspects of Denison's work is contained in the O.E.C.D. publication already referred to. In the course of the conference which was the subject of the publication, each of the general assumptions was questioned. It was contended that the competitive conditions of the model do not hold in practice, that earnings are not determined by marginal productivities, that such productivities frequently cannot be measured, that businessmen do not maximise profits, that economies are never in the equilibrium state posited, and that economies of scale are present which would invalidate the calculations.

Thus, Lundberg, while noting the general range of objections, lays particular emphasis on the neglect of the demand side in the competitive approach. The latter, by assuming continuing full employment of resources, can regard growth as being determined by changes in the supply of productive factors. Changes in demand, leading to under-utilisation of capacity, would result in only short-term variations. Lundberg contends that such segregations between supply and demand factors, must always be artificial. There are inter-relations between the demand and supply conditions in the short-run, and summing up what occurs in a number of short periods gives the long-run results.[10] These short-run fluctuations could mean that incomes were affected by influences other than marginal productivities, hence the former would not necessarily be an accurate reflection of the latter.

Again, Kaldor, commenting on Denison's results, asserts that 'all such estimates are derived from hypotheses concerning the so-called production function and the price system (it is a mild description to call them "strong assumptions") which have no theoretical or empirical basis whatever'.[11] Later when dealing with a specific production function which had been suggested by Svennilson (which had many similar characteristics to, but was not identical with, the type used by Denison) he states: 'there is no reason for supposing that the function is homogeneous in the first degree, let alone of constant unity elasticity, nor that it shifts in time in a neutral manner'.[12] The statement that the function is homogeneous in the first degree refers to its characteristic of constant returns to scale. This characteristic means that the income shares of the factors account for the whole of output. If on the other hand there were increasing returns to scale, so that, for example, a 1 per cent addition of all factors led to a more than 1 per cent addition to output, then estimates based on factor shares would account for only part of the output increase. The reverse would apply if there were decreasing returns to scale. The reference to constant unity elasticity refers to the manner in which one factor is substituted for another. Assuming two factors, for example, a 1 per cent rise in the price of labour relative to capital would, in this case, lead to an offsetting reduction of similar amounts in the quantity of labour relative to capital which would be employed. Thus total spending on labour and capital would remain the same, leaving their relative income shares constant.

Vaizey in his paper lays stress on the complementarity which exists between the inputs in many productive processes.[13] This would lower both the possibilities of substituting one

[10] *The Residual Factor and Economic Growth*, 69.
[11] *Ibid.*, 138.
[12] *Ibid.*, 140.
[13] *Ibid.*, 201–12.

factor for another, and of determining their marginal productivities.

Malinvaud in addition to noting the general theoretical objections, also questioned some of the specific calculations.[14] In the particular case of education, there are several queries which he raised. One concerns Denison's assumptions that the amount of education received by a pupil in a year is proportional to the number of days attendance. Malinvaud points out that when dealing with working hours, Denison had allowed that a cut in the number of hours worked is generally offset in part by an increase in productivity per hour. It is equally feasible that this would apply to education also, since the educational benefits may stem as much from the time a young person spends assimilating what he has been dealing with in school, as from attendance for formal instruction. In addition, the bulk of the increased school attendance affected those who leave school early, whereas Denison's calculations imply a proportional increase for all categories of pupils, which would lead to an overvaluation of this effect. A different point raised was that changes in the type, as distinct from the quantity, of education may be of importance from the viewpoint of economic growth, the expansion in technical education being used as an illustration. Other specific points are also listed in support of Malinvaud's conclusion that Denison had overestimated the measured contribution of education and suggests an estimate of 0·40 to 0·50 per cent in place of the 0.67 per cent per annum growth rate which Denison had estimated. In his conclusion however, he notes that 'externalities' are not covered by such estimates.

Against these criticisms, several counter-arguments were made. Denison's own estimates had shown, as he himself was aware, that all of the conditions necessary for a completely satisfactory application of the classical-type production function were not met. Thus, his data showed that economies of scale had accounted for 0·34 per cent per annum, or more than one-tenth of the total annual growth of 2·93 per cent in the 1929–57 period. Similarly, he had attempted to measure

[14]*Ibid.*, 57–66.

the impact of changes in various restrictive practices, and of underutilisation of labour in agriculture on the measured rate of growth. He accepts then that the theoretical function is only an approximation to reality; the practical question is whether the results which it yields are sufficiently accurate to be useful, or whether they would be hopelessly misleading. Among the specific points of reply he observed that, where short-run disequilibria exist, if the gap between potential and actual output does not vary greatly between the points of measurement, and if the reasons for the gap do not alter, then the contribution made by any factor to actual output will be the same as its potential contribution. He likewise accepts that the elasticity of substitution between factors is probably less than unity, but points to some work which shows that elasticities can vary widely before they have any significant effect on the results obtained.

Johnson in his paper likewise draws attention to the point that the existence of complementarity between factors need not be an insuperable obstacle to the determination of marginal productivities.[15] The substitutability necessary for this determination to occur can be effected through the substitution of one commodity for another, or of one productive process for another, and does not require a marginal adjustment for each specific process. He adds that the 'working out of the marginal productivity principle in the market process is therefore not a simple matter, and must not be expected to reveal itself to casual observation—the economist must be sophisticated in his use of it for analysis'.[16]

The overall result was thus a sharp cleavage of opinions— which was scarcely surprising. As Kaldor had recalled in his paper, criticisms of the classical-type production function have a long history: 'one is reminded of Edgeworth's famous criticism of Wicksteed (who first put forward the proposition that the technological relation between output and input is a "homogeneous function of the first degree"). There is a magnificence in this generalisation which recalls the youth of

---

[15] *Ibid.*, 219–27.
[16] *Ibid.*, 227.

philosophy. Justice is the perfect cube, said the modern sage; and rational conduct is a homogeneous function, adds the modern savant. A theory which points to conclusions so paradoxical ought surely to be enunciated with caution.'[17] If Edgeworth were writing today in full knowledge of all the recent literature on the subject, all that he would need to add are the words 'of constant unity-elasticity' after the words 'homogeneous function'.[18] Denison, on the other hand, commenting on the position adopted by Kaldor (and others) remarked that if, as these criticisms imply, 'everything is simply random, not only my economics but all economics has nothing to offer'.[19]

The purpose in presenting these rather detailed comments on the methods of measurement, and the interpretation of, results regarding the contribution of various factors to increased output, is that the issues involved do not hinge on technical questions, but appear to be much more the results of different value-judgements. As Neild expressed it when summarising the debate, 'it was evident from the discussion that the division between those who believe in the marginal productivity theory of distribution and those who do not was a matter of faith; it was not something that could be resolved by discussion (or conversion)'.[20]

Whatever viewpoint is adopted, the contribution which education makes to economic growth is not something which can be clearly identified and measured. Opponents of Denison-type calculations would obviously adopt this position, while proponents of the marginalist approach accept that 'externalities' would not be caught by such measurements, thus introducing a source of imprecision which might be substantial in the case of any one input such as education.

For present purposes the question is not so much one of precise calculation, but rather whether or not education is a significant factor in economic growth. On this issue a wider

[17]See F. Y. Edgeworth, 'The Theory of Distribution', *Quarterly Journal of Economics*, February 1904.
[18]*The Residual Factor and Economic Growth*, 140.
[19]*Ibid*., 81.
[20]*Ibid*., 273.

degree of agreement seems possible. The Denison measurements suggest that the relative importance of education in this context has varied widely between countries. This difference in relative importance is also echoed in the more general literature on the subject, which suggests that the role of education is one which varies both with time and place. The almost universal conclusion, however, is that it is one which should not be ignored.

CHAPTER 6

THE MANPOWER APPROACH

THE preceding chapters have been concerned with showing how education can have significant economic consequences, which could affect both the individual and social demand for education. These discussions, insofar as they entailed measurement, were naturally concerned with past experiences. If economic factors are to influence educational policies, it is necessary to go one stage further, and examine the possible course of future events, because such decisions as the building of schools, the training of teachers, or the introduction of new courses, are based on predictions about the future patterns of educational needs.

The usual way of linking the economic and the educational patterns is to prepare projections of future employment levels which are then used to derive estimates of the associated educational levels. Given that the future is uncertain, there are inevitable differences of view as to which procedures are most appropriate for the preparation of future estimates.

The choice of method for projections will in part depend on the time period involved. In short-run (under 1 year) and medium-run (up to 5 years) economic forecasts, it is generally assumed that production will be largely dependent on the level and composition of aggregate demand, and the emphasis will accordingly be placed on identifying influences affecting the demand side. Production techniques and the associated labour requirements would be taken as relatively stable. As the time-horizon lengthens, the influence of changes in supply characteristics becomes more important so that in the long run it would be more appropriate to view the output structure as being a product of both demand and supply elements.

The short-run forecasts would be the more manageable

ones, since the degree of change would be smaller and more predictable than for longer-run forecasts. Short-run estimates would be of little use for educational planning purposes, since little reaction can be expected from the educational system over a restricted period. The bulk of the manpower forecasting attempted to date which has been intended for educational purposes has consequently tended to steer a middle course between the two extremes, and to deal primarily with medium-run periods.

The normal procedure in making such forecasts may be thought of as falling into five stages.[1] First, a projection is made of the level of output for the target year(s). Secondly, projections of the expected level of output per worker are prepared, from which, in combination with stage one, the third step of projecting the total number of workers required can be obtained. The fourth stage is to derive the occupational composition of the expected labour force and, finally, the educational level(s) appropriate to each occupation are identified.

In many actual cases the methods adopted may vary from this rather simplified process. In attempting stage four, for example, it is usual first to break down total output and employment into a number of sectors or industries, and then estimate the occupational structure for each industry group. This disaggregation process, as it is termed, is useful because showing the composition of expected output can provide some indication of the consistency of the overall estimates. It sheds light on the pattern of consumer demand which is expected, or for countries which export some of their output, it can show the expected pattern of trade. With some projections, the derivation of occupational break-downs is by-passed, and it is only the educational structure for each industry which is estimated. Where the assumption is that full employment will prevail for the target period, the earlier stages can be reversed in that initially a projection of the labour force is made. The development of output per worker is then projected, and the

[1]The description which follows draws heavily on the description contained in H. S. Parnes, *Forecasting Educational Needs for Economic and Social Development*, O.E.C.D., Paris 1962.

combination of these two determines the total output for the target date. Whatever the precise sequence, the objective of this portion of the exercise may, however, be taken as that of obtaining an estimate of the educational characteristics 'required' by the labour force at the target date(s). This gives a picture of what is termed the 'stock' position at some future date, which can be compared with the stock in the base year. The final procedures are then to estimate the annual flows into and out of the labour force which are expected to take place over the forecast period. This enables the numbers of people 'required' with each type of educational qualification to be estimated on a yearly basis, and thus converts the manpower data into the most appropriate form for educational planning purposes.

II

Given that the basic objective is to prepare estimates of future manpower requirements in a form which will be convenient for shaping educational policies, the immediate problem is to decide how these projections should be made.

Three main methods for preparing projections of output, employment and occupational structures for each industry or sector of the economy crop up most frequently. The first of these, which may be termed the historical approach, consists of analysing data on past behaviour in order to quantify the relationship which existed between aggregate and *per capita* output on the one hand, and the pattern of manpower usage on the other. The presence of a reasonably stable relationship would then permit the projection of such trends into the future. Thus, for example, Verdoorn has suggested that employment shows an elasticity of 0·5 with respect to output —that is, each one per cent rise in output is accompanied by an increase in employment of a half per cent.[2]

The second approach termed the structural, or analogy,

[2]P. Verdoorn, 'Complementarity and long-range Projections', *Econometrica*, 1956.

approach, may take two forms; one dealing only with the home economy, the second related to advanced economies elsewhere. In each case the approach is to compare the pattern displayed by the most advanced sectors with that of other sectors. For projection purposes the usual assumption is that in future years the remaining sectors will tend to reproduce the pattern currently displayed by the most advanced firms or industries.

The third or survey approach, as the name implies, calls for the collection of information from the various firms or sectors as to how they expect output and employment to behave over the forecast period. Information obtained in this way would then be aggregated and checked for internal consistency before being used in the preparation of estimates.

These approaches are not of course mutually exclusive. In some cases all three have been employed, in others various combinations of them, the actual choice made in practice being the result not only of views on the techniques themselves, but also on the type of data, and on the time-span available, for the purpose. To some extent the methods may be regarded as complementing each other since each one has its strength and limitations.

The historical approach, for example, appears to be an essential part of any forecasting process in that a knowledge of past events is a necessary preliminary both to an understanding of the contemporary position, and to forming an appreciation of possible future trends. This appears to be so, whether the methods employed are informed and impressionistic, or systematic and analytical. At the same time the approach gives rise to many difficulties. In the first place the future is unlikely to be a simple extension of the past, so that even the most stable of past relationships is likely to show some alteration over time. A second, and more complex, problem is that there is a difference in the content of past data and of future projections.

The latter are, in the case under discussion, intended to be projections of future demand for manpower. Past data on employment trends refer to the observed interaction of both demand and supply influences, and thus pose formidable

E

problems of interpretation. Past increases in employment of a given category, for example, may be a reflection of an increased supply of such workers, causing a fall in their relative wage, both of which would be consistent with a given demand schedule. Projections, on the other hand, invariably exclude prices (wage-rates), hence any projected growth in employment implies an upward shift in the demand schedule.

In practice, this identification problem, as it is termed, is likely to be even more complex, since output, whether in aggregate or for specific industries, will be changing over time, as will the methods by which output is produced. There will thus be a whole range of influences on both the demand and supply sides of the employment structure. In these circumstances it is not easy to derive much help from the analysis of past trends. Some of the more detailed studies which have attempted to identify the components of productivity increases over time, yield results which are very inconclusive for forecasting purposes. Thus, a study by Kendrick for the U.S. over the period 1899–1953 showed a range of from 0·7 per cent to 5·5 per cent in the average annual rate of increase in total factor productivity for the 31 industry groups considered.[3] For sub-periods of 10 years, significant fluctuations from these average levels were recorded. This variability was as high, or higher in some cases, than the overall rate itself. In addition, the variability did not remain uniform among the various groups.

Measuring productivity in terms of output per man hour makes the position even worse, as the range displayed by the long period was even greater. One conclusion from this study is that productivity movements over time exhibit no simple, regular patterns on which to base forecasts. The inference is that projections based on observed trends in output and employment are likely to be subject to wide margins of error.

This unhappy position could clearly be improved if all, or even some, of the causes of such variations could be identified

[3] J. Kendrick, *Productivity Trends in the United States,* National Bureau of Economic Research, 1961.

and quantified. In the Kendrick study, attempts to do this were made by using research expenditures and measures of the amplitude of cyclical (short-run) fluctuations, as explanatory variables. These measures accounted for about 55 per cent of the observed variability over the period 1919–1953, but they were less successful when applied to shorter time-periods. Of the two, differences in cyclical amplitude were much less important than differences in research spending. Other possible variables which were tried with little success were differences in industrial structure, in the financial strength of industries, and in the proportions of scientific and engineering personnel employed. The most positive result from these attempts was that in the long run research activities apparently help to promote productivity increases, presumably through accelerating the rate of technological change in these industries. This could be an important result for educational forecasting purposes, since such an effect would alter the number and the types of worker needed to achieve any given output. Another U.S. study which yields somewhat similar conclusions is that by Denison discussed in chapter five.[4]

The contribution of advance in knowledge (which may be taken as the product of research activities) had been estimated on a residual basis as accounting for a 0·58 per cent average growth rate over the 1929–57 period, equal to one-fifth of the total growth rate. Within this period the estimates are 0·42, 0·46 and 0·48 for the sub-periods 1929–41, 1941–48 and 1950–57 respectively. For the remaining two year period 1948–50, the estimate shoots up to the staggering level of 2·46 per cent. Denison notes that all studies show a sharp rise in productivity during the early post-war period associated with the recovery in peacetime output, and the modernisation of equipment. Less spectacular, but significant variations are recorded for the other factors analysed by Denison.

The second approach, termed structural, also raises some complex problems. When used within the context of a given industry (so that inferences regarding the future behaviour of most firms are derived from the existing situation of the

[4] E. Denison, *The Sources of Economic Growth in the United States*, Paper No. 13, Committee for Economic Development, New York 1962.

most advanced ones) it results in an incomplete coverage, because this approach does not help to predict the future behaviour of the best firms themselves. Nor does it make any allowance for the entry of new firms. Even for those existing firms which it is supposed to cover, the approach poses such questions as the rate at which they are expected to reach the existing level of the most advanced. Thus, if the 'average' firm is estimated to be at present 10 years behind the most advanced one, should the assumption be that it will take 10 years to close this gap? Or will it take a longer, or perhaps a shorter time than this? On the one hand it could perhaps be plausibly argued that past rates of change must have been slower in less advanced firms, otherwise the differences could not have arisen. This however would appear to depend on an assumption that all firms have equal opportunities and in- centives for taking any given action at one moment in time. Against this it could be contended that in reality, decisions of an investment nature (which are an important element in measures of up-to-dateness) only arise at discrete intervals of time and are determined by the economic lifespan of existing assets. While there will be a spread in the up-to-dateness of firms at any one moment, each firm will not continue to hold the same place in the distribution at all times. Instead, firms will leapfrog each other as re-equipment takes place. An alternative, but related, point would be that even if differences in the age-structure of capital equipment are not significant, differences in management are. To expect that firms would not change their ranking would be to imply that the calibre of management continued to remain relatively unaltered. The longer the forecast period, the more tenuous such an assumption would become. Over a fifteen-year period, for example, about one-third of the male labour-force would retire and be replaced by new entrants. It would be somewhat coincidental, if ability-wise, the distribution of these entrants were to accord with the distribution of those who had retired. Assuming then that changes occur, in the relative calibre of managements, it is possible that there would be associated changes in the relative ranking of any one firm, in terms of its 'up-to-dateness'.

As with so many other aspects, it is not easy to obtain any clear evidence on these points from the available data. The existence of lags in the behaviour of firms has, however, been illustrated by several studies. One U.S. study by Mansfield showed that the average time-lag in the introduction of new production techniques and equipment by firms was 8·2 years, while the range from the most advanced to the 'tail' was about 20 years.[5] The existence of similar lags is likewise pointed out by Salter, who also suggests that one of the main reasons for the lower productivity of U.K. as compared with U.S. firms, does not lie with the leading firms, which tend to be on a par in both countries, but rather in the much higher proportion of plants employing outmoded methods in the United Kingdom.[6] This is a point of some relevance to the later discussion of international comparisons. Salter also suggests that these differences in the existing 'capital' stock will influence both the size and skill content of the required labour-force.

Some evidence on a related point comes from a study by Massell dealing with 19 manufacturing industries in the U.S. over the period 1946–57.[7] This was intended to show whether there was any connection between the industries with the highest initial technological level, and those which experienced the most rapid technological advance during the period. The results were negative, suggesting that sectors with the highest past productivity are not necessarily the areas which will continue to achieve the highest gains. This data is not directly related to the problem under discussion, which is one of the relative positions of firms within industries, rather than of industries within the overall economy.

In so far as firms are concerned there is some evidence to suggest that relative positions are more stable, and are positively associated with size. In another study Mansfield shows that larger firms are more likely to innovate than smaller ones.[8] The notion that big firms, because of greater financial

[5]E. Mansfield, *Industrial Research and Technological Innovation*, New York 1968.
[6]W. E. G. Salter, *Productivity and Technical Change*, Cambridge 1960.
[7]B. F. Massell, 'A Disaggregated View of Technical Change', *Journal of Political Economy*, December 1961.
[8] E. Mansfield, 'Size of Firm, Market Structure and Innovation', *Journal of Political Economy*, December 1963.

resources and market power, are likely to retain their positions of leadership is one which is supported by many economists. This is not necessarily true in all cases, although Mansfield noted that the steel industry was one exception in his analysis, and in a later study Adams and Dirlam discuss the exception in more detail.[9] They show that the most significant techno-logical post-war development—the oxygen steel-making process, which had been pioneered in Austria in the 1949–52 period—was introduced into the U.S. in 1954 by a firm which accounted for less than 1 per cent of output. It was a decade later before the three major firms followed suit. This example may be merely the exception which proves the rule, but it is one which could be repeated elsewhere. The conclusion is that references about relative positions of firms should not be applied mechanistically.

So much then for the use of the structural approach within industries. The position appears even more complex when this comparative approach is applied on an international basis, where inferences about the future position of the more backward countries are drawn from the existing situation of the more advanced nations. This version has been dis-cussed fully by Hollister who refers to it as the analogy ap-proach.[10] To be valid in a global sense, this assumption that future output and employment for a given income level would correspond to some existing pattern for an economy with the same income level would call for the fulfilment of a rather restrictive set of conditions. First, the future pattern of demand in the poorer country would need to correspond to that at present existing in the advanced area. Secondly, it would be necessary to have knowledge of, and access to, technological processes developing in the same way. Thirdly, it would be necessary for the input combinations to be determined in the same way. Fourthly, it would be necessary to have a rate of capital accumulation with respect to income which was

[9]W. Adams and J. B. Dirlam, 'Big Steel, Invention and Innovation', *Quarterly Journal of Economics,* May 1966.

[10]R. G. Hollister, 'Economics of Manpower Forecasting', *International Labour Review,* April 1964.

similar for the two economies. Finally, it would be necessary either to have no foreign trade, or that both economies should have access to the same markets for goods and services, and the same endowments of resources, so that relative prices vary in the same way in each of the economies as income increases. Were these conditions to be satisfied, a similar distribution of output by sectors to that of the advanced economy would be generated in the poorer area as its income level rises. Such stringent conditions are, however, unlikely to be fulfilled in practice; the expectation, therefore, is that direct analogies between countries are unlikely to be valid.

Before reaching this conclusion Hollister reviews the results of various inter-country studies. He cites one by Chenery.[11] On the basis of a cross-section study of economies at various levels of development, Chenery found that after allowance is made for size, there exists a systematic and well-defined pattern in the sectoral distribution of output with respect to income per head. Despite this, however, the production level in different industries varies on average by about 50 per cent for any given income level. This study also found that changes in supply conditions are more important in explaining the growth of industry than are changes in demand. Only about one-third of the observed deviations from proportional growth is attributable to demand effects related to changes in income levels. While this does suggest the possibility of systematic relationships in supply and income effects it is probable that greater variations would occur if a time-series approach were adopted, since this would reflect the introduction of new products and the decline of old ones.

The Chenery study refers only to variations in output. The next step is to examine variations in inputs, whether in the form of total labour input per unit of output (which would affect total employment) or variation in the skill composition of labour inputs (which would affect the occupational structure for any given employment). Hollister discusses each of these in turn. With respect to the first, he quotes a study

[11]H. Chenery, 'Patterns of Industrial Growth', *American Economic Review*, September 1960.

by Arrow and Hoffenburg which shows that for the most part, the hypothesis of constancy of input coefficients over time is not sustained.[12] A Japanese study dealing specifically with the labour input coefficient in two industries is also quoted, and shows a decline of 24 per cent in three years for one, and considerable but unsystematic variation for the second.

Similarly, another Japanese study dealing with labour productivity over a forty-year period, showed that labour inputs varied not only with time, but in different ways in different sectors. This analysis also found that differences in the growth of labour productivity were significantly correlated with differences in the growth of output; and more importantly for our purposes, that, in those sectors where little or no international trade occurred, the rate of productivity increase was less than would have been expected from this relationship. This would suggest that the employment pattern of an economy will be influenced not only by the pattern of output as such, but also by differences in labour coefficients in 'sheltered' and 'open' industries. The conclusion appears to be that fairly wide variations in the employment level associated with any given level of output are widespread, and may be expected as being typical.

Evidence regarding the third element, namely variations in the occupational composition for any given employment and output level, is much more fragmentary. Hollister suggests that it is intuitively plausible that the elasticity of substitution for high-level skills in many productive processes is quite low. One illustration which he quotes in support of this is a study of the Japanese cotton industry which showed that more unskilled workers were employed because of their lower cost, than in comparable European plants with a given equipment, by running machines at high speeds. It appeared, however, that highly skilled groups did not display any similar type of variation.

Some further information on this point is presented by Hollister himself in a later study, where he examines the data

[12]K. Arrow and M. Hoffenburg, *A Time Series Analysis of Inter-Industry Demands*, Amsterdam 1961.

for four of the countries participating in the Mediterranean Regional Project of the O.E.C.D.[13] This study shows that between these countries there were significant variations, not only in the total employment needed to attain a given output, but also in the occupational composition of this total. Thus, for the transport and communications sector, technical and related workers ranged from 0·3 per cent of total employment in Spain and Portugal to 7 per cent in Greece and 8 per cent in Italy. These variations are not explained by compensating bias in other categories. Thus, in combination, professional and executive staff accounted for 1·3 per cent of the total for Portugal, 1·6 per cent for Spain, 2 per cent for Italy and 2·2 per cent for Greece, so the countries are again in the same general order. Hollister warns against the danger of placing too much weight on these results because of the limitations of the data, but at the very least they have a negative value in that they lend no support to the view that the input co-efficients for any given skills would be fixed by technological requirements.

A point worth noting about this study of Hollister's is that it relates to a small group of countries which are comparatively homogeneous and which therefore might be expected to display similar characteristics. They are all located in the same geographical region; hence they should have relatively comparable access to external markets and other influences. They also enjoy somewhat similar climatic conditions, thus reducing another possible source of inter-country differences in production methods. While differences exist, these areas have not very dissimilar income levels. In short there would be a greater *a priori* expectation that 'analogies' between such countries would be more appropriate than those which might be drawn for other countries in general. The available data on this point seems to reinforce the earlier conclusions that analogies between countries are unlikely to be a reliable basis for manpower projections.

A later study by Layard and Saigal which deals with similar points may also be mentioned at this stage.[14] This enquiry,

[13]R. Hollister, *Technical Evaluation of the M.R.P.*, O.E.C.D., Paris 1965.
[14]P. Layard and R. Saigal in *Journal of Industrial Relations*, July 1966.

using data from the 1960 Censuses of Production for a number of countries, presents a cross-section analysis of the relationship between output levels and labour inputs. The relationships examined were (a) that between output and occupational structure for each sector, (b) that between the educational structure for each occupation and output per worker for the economy as a whole, and (c) that between educational levels in each sector and sectoral output per worker. This latter relationship deals directly with the educational/productivity question, and may be postponed until this aspect is dealt with below. At this stage, our concern is still primarily with the first of these relationships, that between output and occupational structure.

The approach adopted by Layard and Saigal differs somewhat from that used in the studies cited above, in that it is output which is made the dependent variable in their calculations, rather than labour inputs. This means that their analysis is concerned not with the labour inputs used to obtain any specified output, but rather with the output levels which are associated with any given labour force structure. This has the advantage that the data are thereby analysed in a form more suitable for manpower and educational forecasting purposes. For the first of the three relationships examined, that of output and occupational structure in each sector, the results are of some interest. For the economy as a whole, 82 per cent of the observed inter-country variation in manpower structures could be 'explained' by differences in the level of output per worker. For different occupational categories, however, the results show wide variations. Thus, while the professional and technical category records a figure of 83 per cent, this drops to a low point of 25 per cent for sales workers. Again, the sectoral distribution of workers also has a pronounced effect on the results; for professional and technical workers in manufacturing industry the figure is 73 per cent, in agriculture it is 72 per cent, but it drops to a mere 3 per cent in the construction sector. The ability of differences in occupational structure to account for differences in output levels varies greatly both as between occupational groups and sectors of activity. At the same time the significant result for educational planning purposes is that the 'explanation' is best for those categories requiring the longest and most specific forms of education.

The actual form of relationship calculated by Layard and Saigal is also of some interest. A linear relationship is fitted, and the resulting coefficients prove to have lower values than those generally anticipated. Thus, once more using the professional and technical category as an example, the calculated coefficient for the economy as a whole is ·52. The interpretation of this coefficient is as follows: a value of unity implies that the category concerned would remain a constant proportion of the labour force as output expands, a value less than unity implies a decline in its relative size; a value above unity a relative expansion. The calculated value would therefore imply a relative decline in the professional and technical category as the economy expands. In contrast, Harbison in his study for Nigeria, which was part of the Ashby report on 'Investment in Education', assumed that occupations calling for third-level education would grow at a faster rate than total employment, while Tinbergen and Bos take a value of unity for their planning model.[15] As with the other items, the value of this coefficient again varies significantly between sectors. For the professional and technical group, the figure is 1·01 for the industrial sector, 0·8 for agriculture and drops to 0·16 for construction. On the whole the conclusion from this study must be that the possibility of deriving reasonable estimates of occupational/output structures for any one country on the basis of the recorded experiences of others, is a rather limited one; limited to certain occupational groups and output sectors. It may be worth observing that the wider range of variation in construction may possibly be linked with the phenomenon noted in one of the studies quoted by Hollister, namely, that variations in rates of productivity increase between countries were found to be higher in the 'sheltered' as compared with the 'open' industries; and construction is naturally a highly sheltered industry.

[15] J. Tinbergen and H. Bos, 'A Planning Model for the Educational Requirements of Economic Development', in *Econometric Models of Education*, O.E.C.D., Paris 1965.

The third, and final, method of projection suggested earlier was the use of surveys of firms regarding their future plans and expectations. This method first assumes that it is technically feasible to obtain such data; an assumption which is largely justified for developed, but hardly for underdeveloped, countries. Secondly, it requires that the information be evaluated to eliminate internal inconsistencies in the replies. In addition, it is also necessary to decide the relative value which should be attached to the various replies, since it is highly probable that these will vary widely, not only as a result of differences in firms' knowledge, but also as a consequence of differences in managerial competence and attitudes. The usefulness of forecasts from firms on long-run trends is also somewhat questionable, in that the majority of them are more familiar with adapting their input requirements to actual or expected supply conditions, rather than to estimating changes in the supply conditions themselves. Hence, it is probable that with the exception of large organisations, firms operate with somewhat restricted horizons.

The problems associated with projecting future employment patterns are, then, as indicated by the whole of the preceding discussion, formidable. Moreover, this is before any reference has been made to the final, and in many respects the most difficult step, namely, the translation of employment projections into educational groupings. For some occupations this translation is relatively simple; doctors, for example, require a highly specific type of educational preparation. At the other extreme there are categories, such as managers or sales people, who may vary very widely with respect to both the level and type of their educational preparation. In between, there are other occupations where educational backgrounds, though not specifically governed by legal or technological considerations, are nonetheless influenced by traditions or social conventions, so that they change relatively slowly in their educational content.

There is, in short, a spectrum of occupational/educational links ranging from the highly specific to the most vague and ill-defined. Yet, if manpower projections are to be useful for educational planning purposes, it is important that these links be quantified in a systematic and functional way. In principle, the same three types of estimating procedure as were discussed above might be used here also, but in practice the amount of data on the educational characteristics of the labour force, whether for the same country at different time periods, or for different countries at the same time, is minimal. At the present time, it does not appear that time-series or cross-section analyses could yield useful results.

The available data at least provide an illustration of the problems involved, some of which have been discussed by Parnes.[16] One of these is the range of educational character-istics associated with various occupations. Parnes illustrates this point with the following data:

TABLE 6.1

Percentage Distribution of Males, Selected Occupations by Number of Years completed Schooling, U.S. 1950

	Number of years schooling completed					
Occupation	8 or less	9-11	12	13-15	16 or more	All
Authors	3·7	5·8	15·0	28·2	47·2	100·0
Mechanical Engineers	9·1	7·2	16·2	17·0	50·5	100·0
Managers (Manufacture)	14·7	14·1	29·3	18·9	23·0	100·0
Photographers	14·3	18·0	40·8	18·4	8·5	100·0
Salesmen (Manufacture)	14·5	15·5	33·6	20·3	16·0	100·0
Bank Tellers	6·4	11·7	51·1	22·2	8·6	100·0
Carpenters	56·9	21·2	17·4	3·6	0·9	100·0

Source, H. S. Parnes, *op. cit.*, 148.

It will be seen from this table that while there is a pronounced modal (most typical) grouping of education for these occupa-

[16]H. Parnes, 'Relation of Occupation to Educational Qualification', in *Planning Education for Economic and Social Development*, O.E.C.D., Paris 1963.

tions, the disparity is also considerable, so that associating each occupational category with the modal educational level could be seriously misleading. Parnes also makes reference to data for the U.S.A., Canada, France and England and Wales, again for the year 1950, which show that the proportion of a given occupational group who possessed any specified level of education varied considerably. Thus, the proportion of professional and technical workers with 13 or more years of education ranged from 51 per cent to 78 per cent, while for clerical workers the range was from 5 per cent to 20 per cent.

Though not directly dealing with this question, the Layard and Saigal study quoted earlier tends to confirm this picture. The second of the three relationships which they examined, that between output per worker and the educational structure of each occupational group, gave the least satisfactory results of the three, in the sense that the fitted relationship had a relatively low explanatory value. Thus, for degree-level workers, differences in output per head 'explained' only 43 per cent of the observed variation in overall occupational structures. Within occupational groups the figure varied from a low point of 1 per cent for clerical workers to 57 per cent for sales workers. The figure for the professional and technical category was 25 per cent. Similar values and ranges were observed for the secondary-level and primary-level groups, though the results for the latter were the ones which displayed the highest degree of statistical significance. Though not intended to measure such an effect directly, these results are consistent with a situation of wide variations in the educational qualifications associated with given occupations and output levels. They may be taken as a form of circumstantial evidence in support of Parnes' results.

One problem with data contained in studies of this type, is that they refer to the actual educational attainments of workers, whereas the more important information for forecasting purposes would be that relating to required educational levels. Very little data are available on this latter aspect; the only official study of this appears to be one made by the U.S. Department of Labour which is discussed by Eckaus.[17]

[17]R. Eckaus, 'Education and Economic Growth', in *Economics of Higher Education*, Washington 1962.

This study graded a sample of 4,000 jobs according to 'general educational development' and the 'specific vocational preparation' required for each. General educational development was classified into seven levels, each of which was subclassified into three headings of mathematical, language and reasoning development. Similarly, vocational preparation was divided into nine levels. The limitations of such a study will be immediately evident. First, the classification of any one occupation reflects the judgement of the individual who makes it. Secondly, as Eckaus notes, neither the various educational levels nor the vocational training requirements can be readily converted into units of conventional school years. Thus it is not clear how the two types of preparation are to be combined with, or substituted for, one another.

Despite these difficulties the data are the nearest available of the type necessary to specify educational requirements for the labour force, and Eckaus in fact applies them to the U.S. for the census years 1940 and 1950. Making assumptions about the length of education corresponding to each of the general and vocational characteristics, he then applies these to the numbers in each of the occupational groups at these census dates. The results show both the absolute amount of, and the changes in, the schooling 'required' by the labour force at both dates. It should be emphasised that since the same educational level was assigned to each job at both dates, any increases in the amount of education 'required' are a reflection of changes in the occupational structure only, and do not allow for any upgrading in the requirements of the jobs themselves. The results may therefore be taken on balance as understating the changes in requirements which had taken place, since the growth in knowledge would have the effect of lengthening the amount of schooling needed at the later date.

The results are, nevertheless, of some interest. On average the amount of schooling 'required' rose from 9·7 years in 1940 to 10·1 years in 1950, or an increase of about 4 per cent. The amount of vocational preparation rose from 1·26 years to 1·35, or an increase of about 7 per cent. The comparison which Eckaus makes between requirements of college graduates and their actual numbers is also interesting. This shows requirements of persons with 4 or more years of college as being 7·1 and 7·4 per cent of the labour force for the years 1940 and 1950 respectively, whereas the censuses show the actual proportions of these groups as being 5·9 and 7·4 per cent respectively. This implies that in 1940 many people whose job required a college education did not have it, whereas by 1950 a balance had been achieved between requirements and actual supply. Eckaus warns against drawing any firm conclusions from the study because of the rather crude nature of the data, and the probability that there were biases both in the census reporting of individuals and in the evaluation of requirements. The importance of the study lies rather in Eckaus' suggestion that 'the approach can be developed into a method for estimating current requirements for an expanding economy. Though certainly imperfect, the method can provide a more concrete basis for educational policy than any heretofore available'.[18]

At the moment we need not enquire into the validity of this claim, but may simply note that such data do not exist for other countries, hence the problem of deriving educational requirements for the labour force in these countries remains. One other possibility discussed by Parnes is to survey employers regarding the educational levels which they in fact, or would wish to, impose when hiring workers. This approach would present the same problem of interpretation noted earlier, but the method would, in this instance at least, have the advantage of referring to current occupational/educational links, whereas census data governing the entire labour force are dominated by past experience, since on average education for the existing labour force would have ceased more than twenty years earlier. While efforts of this type could undoubtedly improve the position, the education/occupation link is the one about which least is known both as regards its present structure and past development.

III

Before reviewing the problems associated with each of the forecasting techniques, it may be useful first to examine some

[18]Eckaus, *op. cit.*

examples of how manpower projections have been made in practice. Descriptions of the procedures in France, Holland and Sweden are contained in a report of an O.E.C.D. seminar which dealt with this question.[19]

In France, employment forecasting is undertaken as an integral part of overall economic planning. Institutional arrangements are co-ordinated with those of other planning activities. The usual planning period is a medium-term one of four to five years. In making employment projections each of the three methods described above is used at different stages. Global trends in employment in each major sector of activity are plotted for ten or so countries over periods up to fifty years. About 25 sectors are used for this purpose. The distribution of manpower by sector of activity in future years can then be estimated either by projecting the trend or by noting the position on the curve of technically more advanced countries. This method combines some elements of both the historical and the structural approach. More detailed studies are then made for each sector by specialist committees. These take account of such factors as technical progress, and changes in working hours and conditions, in arriving at their final estimates. This method is essentially the same as the survey approach, but without a formal survey of the firms concerned in each industry.

It was recognised, however, that these medium-term forecasts were not of much assistance for educational planning purposes, and in 1960 a special sub-committee was set up, which makes longer range forecasts of up to twenty years designed to cope with this problem.

Comparison of the forecasts and of the actual outcome for the earlier four-year plans shows that the rate of productivity change per worker was underestimated, so that output projections were too small. The degree of error in the estimation of employment was, however, much lower, both in aggregate and within each sector. Were this to hold generally it would suggest that employment forecasts could be made which would have an acceptable degree of accuracy. Unfortunately, no details of the

[19]*Employment Forecasting*, O.E.C.D., Paris 1963.

occupational changes which accompanied these output and employment movements are available. Fourastie (the author of the French paper) concludes that the estimates, in spite of their shortcomings and errors, were preferable to none at all.

Forecasting in the Netherlands is based on more formal econometric methods. The short-run estimates, which need not be discussed here, were based on a 36 equation econometric model of the economy. Longer-run forecasts are based on simpler models. A survey made in 1955 for the period up to 1970 used a model which assumed constant elasticities with respect to total output for both employment and capital stock. In addition to aggregate projections of this type, estimates are also prepared for single occupational groups, such as doctors or technicians, which need long training periods. It is not considered worthwhile to do this for unskilled or similar occupational categories, because it is felt that labour supply can adapt itself with sufficient rapidity in these cases. The projections for these individual categories are all based on refined extrapolation of past trends. Thus, in a study of doctors' needs, regional differences were taken into account when estimating the rate at which demand for medical services would rise in response to increased incomes. The demand for physicists—many of whom are engaged in research—was estimated by comparing past trends in numbers with those for groups which had displayed similar rates-of-increase in earlier time-periods. Demand for engineers was estimated by plotting past relationships between their number and the size of national income, and also the trend in their numbers as a proportion of the total labour force. Despite the more formal forecasting methods used, and their incorporation into overall economic models, manpower projections in the Netherlands are done on an informal basis and longer-term forecasts are not part of any regular planning activity as such, unlike the French situation.

In contrast to both of these are the Swedish manpower projections. In the first place, no formal economic plans are produced in Sweden, so there can be no question of forecasting the manpower requirements of specific output targets. Secondly, and more interestingly for our purposes, 'manpower forecasting was started to meet the immediate needs of educational planners'.[20] Because of this, attention was initially focussed on the highly qualified groups of manpower which required a long and specialised training.

Forecasts for these groups were made independently of each other, but gradually the basis is being laid for a more comprehensive system which will ensure a reasonable measure of consistency in the results. A preliminary classification with 300 groups has been developed for educational categories. This, when allied to the usual industrial classification of 50 groups and an occupational classification of 300 groups, would give a possible number of 4·5 million elements. In practice the bulk of these categories would be empty, so that the effective number of industrial/occupational/educational categories is expected to be of the order 10,000–20,000. Pending the development of this integrated system, global estimates were prepared on an ad hoc basis, which could be used for assessing the consistency of sectoral projections. These sectoral projections were largely based on an analysis and extrapolation of past trends, modified where necessary for any known or planned future developments.

Manpower forecasts, which like the Swedish ones were specifically developed for educational planning purposes, have also been prepared in other countries as part of projects sponsored by O.E.C.D. For each of the six countries, Greece, Italy, Portugal, Spain, Turkey and Yugoslavia, participating in the Mediterranean Regional Project, manpower projections were prepared for the period up to 1975, as part of a programme for assessing their educational needs and formulating appropriate policies to meet them. The procedures used need not be discussed since they followed the lines indicated in the Parnes document described at the outset of this chapter. Variations from this sequence naturally occurred in each individual case, mainly due to differences in the amount and nature of available data. Some of the results of these studies as commented on by Hollister have already been referred to in the earlier discussion of this chapter.

As part of a second O.E.C.D. project dealing with the northern European countries, somewhat similar manpower projections have been made for Austria and Ireland. In the

[20]S. Doos in *Employment Forecasting*, 26.

Austrian case one of the interesting departures in the light of the discussion of earlier chapters was the separate treatment accorded to professional and technical workers. The bulk of the projections were based on a typical co-ordination of the historical and analogical approaches—an extrapolation of past trends coupled with comparisons for other O.E.C.D. countries over a 60 year period. The results which these projections yielded for the professional and technical categories were, however, rejected because they did not appear to take adequate account of impending or probable changes in the structure of the economy. A separate projection for these categories was consequently developed which assumed a break with past trends, and laid emphasis on the need for accelerated growth in the numbers of research personnel, engineers and managerial categories.

The manpower projection for Ireland, while following the general procedure, differed somewhat from the pattern of the other O.E.C.D. countries, in that separate projections of output and employment had been prepared as part of an overall economic programming process, somewhat akin to that of the French. The educational planning team had to deal with the final stages of deriving the occupational structure and the associated educational pattern. One way in which the estimates obtained differed from those elsewhere was that in the Irish case educational requirements were estimated not for the total number of people in the labour force at some future date, but only for the inflow of expected new entrants over the forecast period. This was designed as an attempt to cope with the wide range of educational qualifications associated with any given occupation, as exemplified by the U.S. data quoted above. Part, at least, of this spread is due to age differences, since the educational background of people who entered an occupation anything up to 50 years ago might differ significantly from the qualifications expected of current entrants.

All of these O.E.C.D. studies were either wholly or partly the result of ad hoc teams. In most cases, however, some continuing machinery for the preparation of manpower projections in a form appropriate for educational planning purposes has been introduced.

IV

The brief description of the various manpower projections which have been attempted to date is sufficient to show that such forecasting is still in its infancy, and that no country has yet developed its methods to what could be considered a satisfactory level. There is also little scope for detailed comparisons between the forecasts and actual events; nor would there be much relevance in such comparisons since existing techniques are likely to be rapidly superseded. Any discussion of the usefulness or relevance of manpower forecasting for educational purposes may consequently be confined to the more theoretical aspects.

The earlier discussion yielded rather pessimistic conclusions on the possibilities of accurately relating educational, occupational and output levels to each other. In these circumstances the first question might well be whether attempts to project future relationships are useful or necessary. Even on this question the range of available opinion is wide, as the following excerpts taken from the same issue of one journal illustrate:

> The economist admits that skilled manpower is no less rare a commodity than capital, and that it needs more than the compensating mechanisms of the employment market to achieve the optimum balance between skilled manpower supply and demand. . . . Manpower planning is thus seen as a vital element in a rational policy of balanced economic and social development.[21]

> The purpose of manpower forecasting is to facilitate the making of plans for matching the supply and demand for manpower. . . . If there had been accurate manpower forecasting in the past, the anomaly of 'educated unemployed' in countries crying out for high-level manpower, with other qualifications might have been avoided.[22]

[21]M. Debeauvais, in *International Labour Review,* April 1964.
[22]F. Paukert, in *International Labour Review,* April 1964, 339–40.

In an important sense the notion of 'forecasting' supply and demand (for manpower) and marrying the results, is intellectually inconceivable, because the market exists precisely to do that . . . nevertheless it is useful to guess what is likely to happen . . . most economists would take a middle way between the two extremes. Forecasting is necessary and must be done, if growth is not to be held back by shortages of skill. Yet to assume that the market must be ignored is to be too uneconomic.[23]

The greatest lack in the path towards effective manpower forecasting is the almost complete lack of adequate statistical sources . . . but even if the methodological path towards the goal of useful forecasts were clearly indicated—and we cannot claim even this achievement—the journey along that path would still be a difficult and lengthy one.[24]

This range of views, from the clear acceptance by Debeauvais to the partial agnosticism of Hollister, may not seem very great, and it would in fact be possible to quote more extreme views for each position. The intention, however, is to show that even among those who have been active in this area for some time, the role and usefulness of manpower forecasts are still matters of belief rather than of knowledge. These differences of belief may account perhaps for the differences in emphasis on the various aspects. Thus Debeauvais suggests:

international comparisons of employment structure provide the most valuable indications for the developing countries since . . . (domestic) . . . chronological series are generally not available. Moreover, past trends are less important than the structural changes which planning proposes to bring about. Employment distributions observed in more advanced countries can thus be considered as an objective.[25]

[23]J. Vaizey, in *International Labour Review*, April 1964, 354–5.
[24]R. Hollister, in *International Labour Review*, April 1964, 395–6.
[25]Debeauvais, *art. cit.*, 328.

In contrast Hollister states:

> the ... analysis provides very little evidence to support the hypothesis that all economies will follow closely similar patterns in the growth path of the occupational distribution of their labour force. It would seem that any impressionistic type of manpower planning based on such a hypothesis must be regarded with some scepticism.[26]

Or again Debeauvais suggests:

> until such time as progress in research can lead to operational introduction of manpower skills in economic calculation, manpower planning is restricted to the more modest aim of estimating the minimum, rather than the optimum, resources to be directed to training purposes in order to safeguard economic planning targets.[27]

Against this, writing on the same point, Hollister suggests:

> setting lower limits to required levels in certain skills for particular productive processes, seems reasonable intuitively since it seems likely that there are limits to the elasticity of substitution of 'crucial' skills in any complex productive process . . . it is difficult to know, however, a priori, whether or not minima defined in this way would be so low as to be 'uninformative'. This possibility—that the 'requirements' finally derived by means of this analysis would be too limited to be useful—remains a major weakness of this method.[28]

These quotations are sufficient to indicate that manpower forecasting is a technique which cannot be applied mechanistically to questions of educational planning. They might be taken to indicate that the technique cannot be applied at all.

[26] Hollister, art. cit., 378.
[27] Debeauvais, art. cit., 318.
[28] Hollister, art. cit., 380.

An attempt to redress this imbalance may, perhaps, be made by referring to some suggestions which have been put forward to overcome the difficulties which exist.

One possibility discussed by Hollister is the use of cross-section analyses for similar industries in different countries, as a basis for data on substitution possibilities. The reasoning in support of this is that technological knowledge in the pure sense may be regarded as a free international good, so that inter-country differences due to this element should be negligible. This would imply that any observed differences between countries in the occupational composition of given industries could be ascribed to differences in supply conditions. These would indicate whether in practice there was any indication of substitution between labour and other inputs.

The implications which knowledge of this sort would have for manpower forecasting fall into two categories. If, on the one hand, elasticities of substitution turn out to be low, especially for categories involving long educational preparation, then manpower planning research can be concentrated on the deter-minants of technological change, and on the relationships between such changes and the changes in skilled manpower requirements. If, on the other hand, elasticities of substitution prove to be high, the situation would be more complex, since there will be a range of occupational patterns which could be used to produce any given output. Theoretically, if all the information were available the 'least cost' occupational pattern needed to produce any given output could then be determined.

To obtain meaningful results from this approach will not be an easy task, as Hollister is the first to recognise. Simple com-parisons between countries might, for example, reveal signifi-cant variations in the size and occupational composition of the labour inputs used to produce a given output, implying that the substitution possibilities were quite high. But this result could be obtained even if the coefficients were in fact quite rigid for any one production method, and in cases where international differences in the application as distinct from the knowledge of production methods were important. Earlier in this chapter evidence was quoted on the existence of lags in the introduction of new techniques, which would suggest that international variations in the application of new methods could be substantial. Elaborate data and careful analysis would consequently be necessary in order to disentangle such influences and arrive at useful results.

An alternative attempt to cope with these problems is to seek the simplest forms of relationship which will yield useful results. Examples of this form of approach would be the type of relationship used in the preparation of forecasts of engineers in both Sweden and Holland. In each of these instances it was found that there was a comparatively stable relationship between the growth in engineering personnel on the one hand, and the growth in national output on the other. While no one would suggest that either factor was the direct cause of the other, nor deny that various other factors would influence both elements, the justification for using a simple approach of this sort is the purely pragmatic one—that it yielded useful results. Similarly, the Kendrick study noted above showed that the greater the degree of aggregation, the greater the stability in the rates of productivity advance in different industries, which would lend some support to the making of highly aggregative projections.

Only limited attempts have so far been made to apply this more aggregative approach to the educational aspects of manpower forecasting. One of these is the Layard and Saigal study, already mentioned. Apart from the two-stage approach discussed earlier (occupation by sector and education by occupation), this study also dealt with the direct relationship between educational levels and output per head in each sector. Though the calculated coefficients for this section did not have a very high explanatory value, the results may be considered reasonably satisfactory in that they were statistically significant for each educational level. Thus 66 per cent of the observed differences in the proportions of degree-level workers for the economy as a whole could be 'explained' by differences in output, while for secondary and primary education the figures were 47 per cent and 45 per cent respectively. Again the variations by sector were very large; from a low, in the case of those with secondary education, of 2 per cent in construction, to a high for the same group, of 63 per cent in services. It is important to record, however, that since 'output' in the services sector is mainly measured from the input side, this would account for part of the closer observed relationship between labour inputs and output for this sector.

Another attempt at applying an aggregative approach is found in a Swedish study for the period up to 1980.[29] This study treated changes in the demand for educated personnel as a function of two factors: the level of employment in each sector, and time. The reasoning given in support of this approach is somewhat as follows. Changes in overall demand for educated people may be thought of as arising in two ways: first, through changes in the relative size of different industries which vary in the educational composition of their labour force at all periods of time, and secondly, through changes in the proportion of any given industry's labour force possessing any given level of education. In making the projection to 1980 a separate estimate of employment in each sector was used, which means that the output and labour productivity patterns were taken as autonomously determined. Data for the period 1930–60 was analysed to determine the rate of change that had occurred in the educational composition of employment in each sector. These rates were then projected for the period up to 1980. The resulting estimates of total requirements of educated people are thus a combination of an autonomous output projection for the demand side, and a time-series extrapolation of the supply side. They are of a rather limited type, since the effects of changes in supply characteristics are limited to altering the characteristics of the labour force, but not their performance.

Some of the limitations of this approach are evident. To assume, for example, that past trends in the relationship between demand and supply of educated people will continue is to assume the answer to some of the questions on which information is most needed. Similarly, to assume that output is independent of the educational composition of the labour force is to assume both that education has no direct effect on productivity and no effect on the composition of output,

[29]O. Milstam, *Demand for Labour of Different Educational Categories in Sweden up to 1980*, O.E.C.D., Paris 1964.

matters which are again subjects of debate. Milstam himself also refers to another limitation, namely the absence of any price or wage data.

Despite these shortcomings, the approach is of interest as an attempt to formulate hypotheses which are simple, and which may nonetheless yield usable results. In this respect, such attempts may perhaps be likened to early attempts at formulating the relationship between income and consumption spending, and like these latter approaches may be expected to be refined and improved upon as new knowledge and data become available.

While some improvements may be expected in the field of manpower projections, it would be unrealistic to assume that any forecasting procedure can ever be developed which enables the course of future events to be accurately predicted. Any forecasting procedure is more appropriately viewed as an attempt to assemble the relevant information which will facilitate rational decision-taking in the face of uncertainty. The time-lags which characterise the educational system require that some view regarding the future be included when decisions to commit teachers, buildings and other resources to specific purposes are being made. Manpower projections are one way of attempting to have economic considerations in the shape of future employment needs incorporated into this activity. Whether they represent the best or most appropriate method of doing so, is still an open question.

CHAPTER 7

EFFICIENCY IN EDUCATIONAL PROVISION

APART from the wider aspects discussed in the preceding chapters, a further question of considerable importance from an economic viewpoint is the efficiency with which the resources allocated to education are utilised. As was the case with these earlier discussions, it will again be seen that this efficiency question is rendered complex because of the special characteristics associated with educational provision.

With products channelled through a market process, efficiency problems are dealt with by the normal working of competitive forces. Efficiency is normally thought of as minimising the cost of producing any given output. In a competitive environment firms must strive to achieve cost-minimisation, because failure to do so would lead to competitors being able to sell at lower prices and thus ultimately force the inefficient firm out of business. It should be noted that this pressure for efficiency not only entails the minimisation of cost for a given output, but also ensures the selection of both the most efficient output level and product type. Thus a firm which had secured the minimum attainable cost for a given output level, might still be underpriced, because at some higher level of output economies of scale were possible which resulted in lower cost per unit of output. Again, a firm with the least cost and correct scale of output might find itself in difficulties if its product did not possess the correct characteristics, for example, producing black motor cars for consumers seeking coloured ones.

In principle, these efficiency questions could also be dealt with in the educational case by the use of a competitive system. Teachers' salaries could be determined by schools bidding for personnel; this process would not only determine the number of teachers who would be hired, but would also allocate them on a quality basis among the schools, since the better calibre teachers would command the higher salaries. Similarly, the location of schools would tend to respond to population movements affecting the level of demand. In the short-run, differential prices might be used to cope with this problem, in that schools experiencing increased demand could afford to raise charges, while conversely, schools located in areas of declining population might lower them in order to retain or attract pupils from outlying locations. In the longer run, new schools would be located in areas of expanding population, while older ones in the declining areas would close. Changes in production methods or in the form of educational product would take place in a similar way. A new technique which enabled a given education to be provided at a lower cost—whether of time or money—to the student would be introduced by some schools to whom it would give a short-run advantage, thus compelling others to follow suit in the longer run.

In principle then, many of the efficiency questions in education are susceptible of resolution along the usual competitive lines. But some would still remain. The typical pattern of population distribution, with high density urban and lower density rural areas, would mean that in many cases students would have little effective choice of schools. This potential monopolistic power thereby conferred on schools would be strengthened by imperfections in knowledge on the part of many pupils and parents concerning the characteristics of the education available to them. Even in the context of a competitive-type market system, efficiency problems might still persist with education.

In practice, the efficiency aspects of education are complicated by the presence of public sector financing or provision of schooling. It has been seen in the earlier chapters that there may be a multiplicity of objectives underlying such public sector activity. There will also be some divergence between the private and social allocation of the costs and benefits associated with such education, coupled with differences in the relative valuations attached to various effects. Given the existence of these ambiguities in the definition and measurement of the output or 'product', it follows that any assessment of 'efficiency' in provision becomes more nebulous and more complex.

Such problems are by no means unique to education, and the general question of efficiency in public expenditure is one which after decades of comparative neglect had begun to receive considerable attention from economists in recent years. An examination of the resulting literature, with its use of 'output budgeting', 'cost-effectiveness', 'systems analysis', 'efficiency auditing', and similar phraseology, might suggest to the uninitiated that a variety of methods had been developed for the treatment of this question. The differences in nomenclature, however, primarily refer to the scale or the context within which a particular problem is being tackled, and should not mask the underlying unity in the basic approach.

Essentially, the approach adopted is one which seeks to identify the 'output' or 'objectives' of each expenditure programme in a measurable way, and then to determine the cost patterns associated with the attainment of these outputs. In the absence of a market for the product or service in question, each aspect of the 'efficiency' question must be systematically analysed and evaluated. It is important to emphasise that in these contexts, efficiency is thought of as the minimisation of cost for an appropriately defined output, which should not be confused with cost-minimisation in any absolute sense. The aim is not that of identifying the 'cheapest' way of providing a product or service, because the cheapest system might provide an inappropriate and hence inefficient output. The analogy might be made with some market product, such as motor cars, where the provision of only the cheapest model would not be the most 'efficient' way of meeting consumers' requirements for road passenger vehicles, since many of them would be willing to pay the higher prices needed for safer, faster or more luxurious vehicles.

It will be apparent that the definition of appropriate output or objectives for public sector activities is one of the crucial stages in any efficiency oriented analysis. Many, if not all, of the items concerned are like the motor car illustration, in the sense that the characteristics associated with different methods of meeting any given requirement not only affect the cost, but also the nature of the output obtained. Different types of missiles to meet a 'requirement' for defence purposes will, for example, be likely to differ in speed, range, reliability, manoeuvrability and other respects. To determine the most 'efficient' weapon in these circumstaces calls for a very careful definition of the relevant defensive objective(s), including the scale involved, since the system which is most efficient at one scale need not be so at another. Similarly, in the provision of a health service, the mode of treatment (e.g. hospital versus out-patient), length of treatment, waiting time by patients and similar characteristics are all items which would require careful definition in attempts at measuring efficiency of provision.

In the particular case of education, the relevance of this efficiency approach and its difference from a simple cost analysis can be illustrated by taking some of the public sector objectives suggested in chapter two. One of these might be described as the provision of minimum facilities to all specified children. For illustrative purposes this might be taken as the introduction of compulsory education for a given number of years, calling for the provision of schools, teachers and related equipment. The actual pattern of provision—number and size of schools, number of teachers etc.—in such instances would, in part, reflect the size and distribution of the relevant population, but also the administrative procedure specified. Comparative costings for such a system are typically made on the basis of expenditure per pupil, and could then be prepared to throw up any cost differences associated with variations in school size, area or pupil characteristics. To continue the illustration it may be assumed that these show the cost per pupil to be lower in large schools than in small schools, because of the larger number of pupils per teacher in the former. When considered solely in terms of cost minimisation for the educational budget, such data would suggest that larger schools were preferable.

To decide whether this would be true or not in 'efficiency' terms, would require much further information. Even if there is no limit (other than the physical capacity of the buildings concerned) to the number of pupils who may be taught by one teacher, and if the relevant objective is merely to ensure that all pupils have access to a teacher, it is still unlikely that large schools would be the most 'efficient' solution for all pupils. Given the scattered population of rural areas, it would be necessary to enrol pupils from a wide area to fill a large school. But in many instances this would entail costs in time and transport. In terms of the total cost per pupil (inclusive of all such items), small schools might be less costly than larger ones, even though the 'within-school' costs (buildings, teachers etc.) of the latter might be lower. However, it is total costs which would be relevant to the determination of an efficient solution.

More typically, some administrative procedures would be used to further define the nature of the required objective. A common example is the specification of pupil-teacher ratios, which indicate the maximum and minimum numbers of pupils to be catered for by a teacher. Regulations of this nature permit smaller numbers of pupils per teacher in the smaller schools in order to compensate somewhat for the teacher having to cope with a much wider age-spread in his pupils. This contrasts with larger schools where numbers are sufficient to permit some degree of teacher specialisation. It may be noted that in addition to defining some limits to the range within which costs per pupil may vary between schools, rules of this type may also take on the role of objectives in their own right. A low pupil-teacher ratio, for example, may become an indicator of the quality of the facilities provided, in which case the large schools with the higher ratios may be the most inefficient in terms of achieving this 'quality' objective. While attempts to introduce quality or other characteristics into the definition of the desired objective represent a movement in the relevant direction, simple pupil-teacher ratios still relate to the 'inputs' available to the pupil, hence they only give an indication of the quality of the 'output' (in terms of education received by the pupil) on the assumption that there is a direct relationship between inputs and outputs.

The movement towards a specification of objectives in output terms might be made by including some measure of pupil attainment in the prescribed minimum level of facilities. Such an attainment measure will call for the specification of some curriculum and secondly, for some evaluation of the pupils' performance, whether by formal examination, teacher assessment or other means, in relation to this course. Apart from the obvious complexities of defining appropriate attainment measures, the identification of the most efficient pattern of provision will be further complicated by the need to take account of the variations in pupil achievement which will occur. Examination results, for example, show a wide range of pupil performance, from passes with distinction down to abject failure. If the output objective is simply specified in terms of pupils passing the specified examination, then in effect every school will be 'inefficient'. Pupil failure at examinations would indicate failure to attain the prescribed minimum, but pupils scoring high marks well in excess of the pass level could be taken as a 'waste' of resources because a mere pass level of performance could presumably have been attained with a reduced amount of teaching. For efficiency evaluation, then, it would be necessary to specify the range of pupil attainments desired, before schools could be evaluated in a meaningful way.

The illustration could be extended but by now the basic point should be clear, that assessments of efficiency in education cannot be made solely on the basis of cost data, but must also take account of the relevant output objectives. In education, these latter can be highly complex, with the result that objectives are sometimes specified in terms of 'inputs' (teachers, schools etc.) rather than in terms of 'output' (educational achievement by pupils). It will be apparent that the definition of appropriate objectives is not a task which can be undertaken by economists, nor by any other single profession, since the range of relevant factors encompasses many facets of human behaviour. Not surprisingly, therefore, there have been few attempts at comprehensive efficiency analyses of education. However, some partial attempts have been made which will serve as convenient methods for illustrative purposes.

F

II

An illustration of an efficiency study dealing with an objective of the 'minimum level of facilities' type is contained in one of the O.E.C.D. country studies referred to in chapter six.[1] This contains an analysis of the costs per pupil associated with categories of 'national school' (schools catering for the bulk of the compulsory education), together with an attempt to relate these to possible output objectives.

The cost portion of the analysis showed that there were significant differences in current and capital costs between the various school sizes. Teaching costs, for example, were three times as high in the smallest as compared with the largest schools. The question was, then, whether the existing pattern represented the most efficient method of attaining the desired objective(s) of the national school educational programme. Official descriptions of objectives were of little help for this purpose, being either too general or inappropriate. One official description, for example, says their intention is to provide a certain minimum standard of education for all children between the ages of 4 and 14 years. Curricula and a terminal examination (which the majority, but not all, of the children sat) were specified for these schools, which would have provided the basis for some measure of pupil success in attaining the specified minimum standard. But no attempt was made to evaluate the system in this way. In part, this was due to the incomplete coverage given by available data, but also because a measurement in these terms would have shown all schools to be 'inefficient', for the reasons outlined in the illustration given above.

The solution adopted in this Irish study was for the group itself to specify possible output objectives and use these as the basis for illustrative analyses. Four measures were taken: first, the apparent length of time taken by pupils to cover the specified curriculum; secondly, the proportion of students who obtained scholarships to post-primary schools; thirdly, the

[1]*Investment in Education*, Dublin 1965.

curriculum available; and fourthly, the range of facilities associated with each category of school. The actual choice of measures was influenced by the type of data which could be obtained in the time available, but they were intended to illustrate various types of potentially relevant objectives.

The first measure, the apparent time taken to complete the prescribed course of instruction, would need to be conducted on a cohort basis in order to obtain correct results, that is by taking a group of pupils at the point of first entry to school, and then following through their school progress up to completion. Since the full course of instruction was an eight-year one, this cohort approach could not be adopted. Instead a cross-section analysis was made of all the pupils in one year. The typical age of entry was 5, so that a pupil making regular progress should be commencing the second year of the course at age 6, the third year at age 7, and finally completing the course at age 13. All pupils were then classified on this basis, into those who were in the expected grade for their age, those who were 'advanced' (being in a higher than expected grade), and those who were 'delayed' (those in a lower than expected grade). Even for pupils in the first grade, a distribution of this type was, as expected, obtained, because children enter school at varying stages between the ages of 4 and 6. Again, as expected, it was the small schools which had the greatest proportion of 'delayed' pupils in this first grade, because these are predominantly rural schools, and it is rural children who on average enter school at the later ages. The data for each of the subsequent grades showed a steady increase (in the order of 30 per cent) in the proportion of 'delayed' pupils as the senior grades were reached, which may be taken as reflecting the proportion of pupils who had to repeat a grade. The rate of increase between the first and higher grades was similar for each type of school. This meant that the absolute proportion of 'delayed' pupils was higher in each grade for the smaller schools, because of their initial higher proportion, and was associated with later entry. The pattern for the later grades could be interpreted as meaning that irrespective of age of entry, the probability of having to repeat at least one year of the course was broadly comparable for each type of school.

One of the relevant cost-effectiveness questions arising from this would be whether it would be cheaper to spend more in efforts to have a larger proportion of the children complete the course in the standard period, rather than incur the cost of additional years of schooling. For its immediate purpose, that of comparing the efficiency of the various schools' sizes, the study could be taken as yielding relatively neutral results, with the bias, if any, against the smaller schools.

The second measure used, the proportion of children from each school type who won scholarships to post-primary education, showed that the pupils from the larger schools had much higher success rates relative to those from smaller schools. This information would be relevant not so much to the question of the efficiency of primary education itself, but rather to a different objective of the 'equality' of access type, since it would imply that for low income groups to whom scholarship aid would be important, attendance at smaller schools would weaken their prospects for further education.

The third measure—curriculum available—showed that the range of subjects available in the smaller schools was more restricted than that of their larger counterparts. Following the usual welfare arguments that a wider range of choice represents a superior position, this could be used to suggest that the pupils of the smaller schools were worse off in this respect.

The fourth measure—facilities available—which dealt with a range of items from equipment, libraries, special study or recreational rooms, right through to structural data on such things as heating and lighting, again showed the smaller schools to be worse off. Part of these differences could be attributed to age, since the smaller schools were on average older, but a significant fraction were not. These measures were used as indicators of school environment, the usual reasoning being that the richer the environment, the better the pupil performance.

The conclusion from this Irish study was that there was a prima facie case for altering the pattern of school size and location in the direction of larger schools, since the small schools had much higher costs per pupil and did not appear to be as satisfactory from an output viewpoint. However, given the preliminary nature of the analysis various reservations and qualifications were appended which need not be dealt with here.

This study was concerned with just one facet of an efficiency evaluation, in that it dealt only with the relative performance of different schools within a given curricular and organisational framework. Its conclusions are also qualified by the fact that any of the observed results could not be standardised for the existence of other, especially non-school, influences on pupil performance.

A more comprehensive analysis of the various factors which apparently influence pupil performance within the context of a given school system, is that undertaken in the U.S. as part of the civil rights programmes.[2] The study was initiated as part of an inquiry dealing with the relative availability of equal educational opportunities for all individuals.

One portion of the study dealt with student achievement and the relationships which this bears to school characteristics such as teacher quality, availability of libraries, laboratories and so forth. The first finding from this section of the study was 'that the schools are reasonably similar in the effect they have on the achievement of their pupils, when the socio-economic background of the students is taken into account'. In other words, while pupils in different schools do not reach the same level of attainment, the differences are associated with non-school rather than with school characteristics. However, those differences which did exist between schools were more pronounced in the case of relatively underprivileged pupils; about 20 per cent of the attainment of negroes in the South was associated with their schools, in contrast to about 10 per cent for whites. This would suggest that improvements in school quality would have the largest effect on the underprivileged children.

The school characteristics which contributed to these variations in pupil attainment are also of some interest. A major influence appeared to be the educational backgrounds

[2]*Equality of Educational Opportunity*, Washington 1966.

and aspirations of other students in the school. Thus, the analysis suggests that children from a given family background entering schools whose pupils are drawn from different socio-economic groups will record different levels of achievement. Again this effect was more pronounced for the underprivileged groups. A second factor of somewhat similar importance to pupil achievement was teacher quality, again with the effect more pronounced for the underprivileged. In this case too, the effect was progressively greater at higher grades indicating a cumulative impact of teacher quality on pupil attainment.

Finally, it may be of interest to refer to two factors which were found to have relatively little effect on pupil performance, namely the facilities and curricula of the schools, though again to the extent that they did show some impact it was more pronounced for minority pupils.

The general conclusion is then that school characteristics are relatively unimportant influences on pupil performance, a result which if valid, and generally applicable, would be of relevance in designing efficiency studies. It has, however, been challenged by Bowles and Levin on several grounds.[3] One criticism is that the treatment of expenditure per pupil was defective, because it was based on average expenditure for each school district, hence it was only variations between districts which were recorded in the analysis. Bowles and Levin refer to various pieces of evidence which show that significant variations occur among schools within a district and that these follow a systematic pattern, with the schools attended by underprivileged children recording substantially lower expenditure. The exclusion of these intradistrict variations would consequently lead to an understatement of the effect on pupil attainment of variation in spending per pupil. Moreover, the authors refer to some evidence of variations within schools, and even within a given class, in the amount of resources allocated to various types of student; factors which would further suggest that the report understates the impact of school inputs.

[3]S. Bowles and H. Levin, 'The Determinants of Scholastic Achievement— an Appraisal of some recent Evidence,' *Journal of Human Resources,* Winter 1967.

A second criticism concerns the restricted measurements of school facilities used in the report. The only measure used for pupils in the lower grades was the number of books per student in the school library. For the senior grades a second measure, the presence of science laboratories, was added. Bowles and Levin also criticise the absence of data on class size and past school experiences. The report did use a pupil-teacher ratio based on total pupils and teachers per school, but this was rejected on the grounds that variations in the number of hours of classroom teaching would significantly affect the actual size of class—which is the relevant measure for pupil attainment studies. Past school experience could have been important because the survey was made at the beginning of a school year, when the current inputs would account for relatively less of existing pupil attainment.

Objections were also raised to the manner in which the calculations of the effect which each factor had on attainment were made. A linear regression model was used for this purpose, which assumes that each of the factors has an effect independent of that caused by the other factors, and that the size of the effect produced for each additional unit of the factor does not vary with the total amount of the factor used. The appropriateness of this model for the analysis is challenged on the grounds that several of the factors studied could be interdependent to a considerable extent. Thus it is suggested that background characteristics of students and the characteristics of the schools they attend are highly correlated (poor children attend poor schools). The relevance of this to the survey results is that a statistical measure of the type used will always attribute any joint contribution of factors to whichever of them is analysed first, so that it overstates the contribution of the first and understates that of the second factor. In the survey, student background was the first factor introduced and school resources the second, so that it was the latter whose effect was understated.

A further criticism raised was that the achievement tests used to classify pupil attainment would give an advantage to pupils enrolled in academic, as distinct from vocational or commercial courses; as such they would favour the children from the higher socio-economic groups and would further overstate the effect of student background. Another criticism of the large influence attributed to student background was the restricted measurements of social class, which excluded parental occupation and income, and used only parental education, a measure which can be particularly inadequate for negroes. The conclusion was that the report's findings regarding the ineffectiveness of school factors and the influence of various other factors are not substantiated by the evidence.

These Irish and U.S. examples and the comment on the latter are sufficient to indicate the difficulties in designing adequate measurements for evaluating the efficiency of school provision. These examples, moreover, relate to just one aspect of the overall question of efficiency within education, since they treated the structure of the school system as given. In terms of conventional business analyses this means that they were concerned with exploring efficiency in the context of a given product, given factors of production and given production methods. Hence they were essentially of a static or short-run nature.

One step towards a more comprehensive assessment would be to explore the consequences of introducing any one change into this specified pattern. One such change would be to alter the school structure, an issue of some contemporary interest in many countries. Husen discusses some aspects of this type of change and draws on some interesting Swedish data.[4] The question which he examines is the relative merits of comprehensive as compared with selective type schools. Husen notes that such comparisons are generally made in terms of the end products, that is those who complete the courses of each type of school, whereas an adequate assessment would include students who take or complete only part of a course.

The age at, and methods by which selection is made for higher levels of schooling are one factor which affects the proportions of completers and non-completers. To illustrate this, reference is made to the results of an experiment in

[4]T. Husen, in *Social Objectives in Educational Planning*, O.E.C.D., Paris 1967.

Stockholm. The city was divided into two zones. In one, pupils competed for entry into secondary school at the end of fourth grade, or about the age of 11 plus; in the other zone entry was either postponed to the end of sixth grade, or the schools were conducted on comprehensive lines (that is with no separation of pupils into 'academic' and other schools). By classifying pupils into three socio-economic groups, the results showed that the early selection schools had a much smaller proportion of pupils from the lower social groups in sixth grade (17 per cent) than the later selection schools had in seventh grade (46 per cent).

Husen then explores the way in which these differences came about. A first factor was that a smaller proportion of children from the lower social group who possessed a given level of ability applied for admission to the selective schools. Thus for those pupils who were placed in the top 4 per cent of ability, on the basis of intelligence tests, 87 per cent of those from the highest social group applied for admission to the higher school, 85 per cent applied from group 2, while only 66 per cent from those in group 3 (the lower group) did so. These selective positions held for each of the ability levels, though the gap between the social groups widened as the lower ability levels were reached. Thus, for ability level 5 (the middle or average level) the percentages of applicants from each social group were 70, 47 and 24 per cent, respectively. Despite their lower proportion of applicants, a higher proportion of the pupils from the lower social group had their applications rejected. Thus, for the highest ability level, 13 per cent of applicants from the lowest social group were rejected compared with 6 per cent for each of the other groups. For the average ability level, the variation was less pronounced: 57 per cent of applications from pupils in the lower group were rejected, compared with 60 per cent for group 2 and 50 per cent for group 1. High ability applicants were rejected because the actual selection was made on the basis of schools marks, and while these were (as is usual) fairly strongly correlated with intelligence measurements, they were not identical with them. Husen suggests that this discrepancy between the two is an indicator of social handicap, because school marks reflect the influence of social background to a greater extent than is the case with intelligence tests.

Husen goes on to note that 'screening-out' at the selection stage is not the only way in which pupils from lower social groups are affected by a selective system. Referring to French and British experience as well as to Swedish data, he observes that of those actually admitted to such schools, the failure rates measured in terms of those who dropped out, those who had to repeat grades, or those who failed examinations, were higher for pupils from lower social groups. Accepting that the level of educational attainment for those who complete a selective system is higher than that of pupils who remain in a comprehensive system, the question which Husen poses is: which system has the better total output?

This question can be given different answers, depending on the objectives and the relative importance attached to each objective of educational policy. In economic terms, an answer could in principle be given by the use of rate-of-return, or manpower, data, both of which would indicate the value to the economy of a sharply differentiated series of educational products from the selective system, on the one hand, compared with the more homogeneous flow from a comprehensive system on the other. In non-economic terms the answer would depend on the interpretation accorded, and the value attached to objectives such as 'equality of opportunity'. Since these values, or at least the articulation of them, vary considerably between individuals, groups and nations, no unique answer can be presented to this aspect. Broadly, however, it would appear that the more 'equality' is interpreted in terms of equality of access to education, rather than in terms of equality of pupil attainment, the greater is the value which would be accorded to selective-type systems.

This particular discussion of school structures may be seen then as an illustration of one aspect of the efficiency problem, namely varying the characteristics of the end product. Following the business-type analogies used earlier, it is comparable with deciding whether to produce say, a family saloon type of motor or a high-powered sports car. For business firms this question of product-type would be decided by consumer demand; in the case of education it will more usually be decided through the political process. Whatever the mechanism used for the purpose, it is a question which needs to be resolved before any comprehensive efficiency assessment of an educational system can be made.

A further 'efficiency' question which enters any comprehensive study is that of determining the most effective method for producing the desired output. All of the examples to date have essentially been conducted in the context of the conventional school method with its reliance on 'chalk and talk'. The continued reliance on labour-intensive methods of production in education is in marked contrast to the trend displayed by other industries, which have generally adopted more capital-intensive techniques. In itself this does not mean that the continued use of traditional methods is inefficient; they may still be the best ones available. Nonetheless, it is possible to provide some indication to the contrary.

A first point to establish is that reliance on conventional methods is likely to result in education becoming a more costly product in relation to other goods and services. This is the case with conventional statistical measurements of output and price levels, because in the absence of any accepted output measure, education is valued from the input side for national income purposes. To take the main input, since teachers' real salaries tend to rise in line with overall growth in incomes, this means that costs, whether in aggregate or per pupil, would rise over time.

A more elaborate estimate of the rising cost of education associated with conventional methods is provided by a study of British universities.[5] This dealt with universities at three different points in time, 1938, 1952 and 1962. The basic output measure used was the number of graduates plus unqualified students produced in these years. In addition, these numbers were weighted in three ways, first on an 'educational' basis, where each course was weighted by the length of time taken to complete it, secondly on an 'economic' basis, the weights

[5]M. Woodhall and M. Blaug, 'Productivity Trends in British University Education, 1938-62', *Minerva*, Summer 1965.

being the relative earnings of graduates from the different categories, and thirdly on a 'cultural' basis, where in the absence of other measures, the weights were the reverse of the economic ones.

In this way indices of the output of graduates, both in unweighted and weighted terms, were obtained. The second stage was to construct an index for the inputs used. Teachers' salaries in real terms were obtained by deflating the money payments in each year for the average salary rises which had occurred. The real value of the students' time used in education was similarly calculated by deflating the money earnings of young people for the rise in juvenile wage rates over the period. Estimates of capital and other current inputs were also calculated. The results thus provided a measure of the change in the inputs used by the universities in these years, adjusted for any price changes which had taken place over the period. The index in inputs obtained from these calculations was then compared with the output index in order to calculate the trend in productivity over the period (productivity being measured as output per unit of input), and this showed that for each of the output indices productivity had been falling by about 1 per cent annually for the period as a whole. Put differently this means that a rise of about 1 per cent annually had been taking place in the total inputs needed to produce any given output. The authors point out that this trend of falling productivity runs counter not only to that of manufacturing, but also to the trend of other service industries, and add that all of the efforts of universities appear to be directed towards further reducing measured productivity by, for example, pressing for reduced student-staff ratios.

An obvious objection to this type of productivity measurement is that it fails to capture any quality changes which may have taken place; the relevance of this is that a productivity rise can be used either to raise the volume of output of a given quality, or to raise the quality for a given quantity of output. The authors themselves recognise this limitation, but in the absence of any agreed quality measures are unable to quantify the possible magnitude or even direction of any quality changes.

A somewhat different approach to this question of choice of production methods would be to examine the scope for raising productivity. An extensive discussion of this aspect in the context of higher education is that of Harris who reviews various experiments with the use of television, teaching machines and other mechanical aids.[6] One series of experiments in Pennsylvania State University in 1956–7 showed total costs for four courses using conventional methods to be 75 per cent higher than for televised courses. The cost difference between the two methods varied with student numbers; for small numbers the televised courses were the more expensive, but as numbers rose the positions were reversed.

It is more difficult to evaluate the educational results obtained, since it would be unreasonable to assume that a change in production methods had no effect on the end-product. Harris quotes the results of various comparisons, which show that of 110 cases, 68 favoured television and 42 conventional methods. Of the 38 cases where the differences between the two methods were statistically significant, 29 favoured television. On the face of it, therefore, the results favour the newer technique, but several doubts were still unresolved. One criticism suggested that they measured only the accumulation of information which is but one facet of the total educational process. Again it was suggested that while much material of a purely expository nature can be conveyed more clearly by pictures rather than by words, the students' understanding of the material is likely to be primarily measured in verbal terms.

In addition there are the possible problems created by attitudes of both students and staff towards changes in teaching methods. Students sometimes complained that with television courses, they became spectators rather than participants, that the inability to ask questions of the lecturer reduced the value of the course. Harris quotes the results of one study, however, which showed that 32 per cent of students in one course preferred television strongly enough to leave the large class in the lecture hall and return to the television

[6] S. E. Harris, *Higher Education: Resources and Finance*, Maidenhead 1962.

classrooms. Also of interest was that whereas only 15 per cent of students in the first six rows of the conventional lecture hall preferred television, almost 50 per cent in the last seven rows preferred it. In general the evidence seems to suggest that other things being equal, students prefer conventional methods. The problem of course is that in practice things are not equal. In particular, with television there is the possibility of small numbers of very able teachers being used in place of large numbers of less able ones and here the indications are that students prefer the former to the latter. With the technique still in its infancy it is too early to know which instructional method to use. The data, such as they are, do at least suggest that changes in the conventional methods may be justified on both cost and quality grounds. As the growth of education continues, the case for the more effective use of the most able teachers, whether by television or other aids, will be strengthened. It is likely that more effective use will be made of television's technical possibilities. Harris quotes one observer as remarking that so far there has not been any televised instruction, but rather instruction televised.

Similar remarks could apply to other devices, such as teaching machines, tape recorders etc.; hence it is not necessary to discuss each of these separately. The intention here has been to illustrate the nature of the economic choices which must be made when deciding to provide educational courses.

Apart from the question of using capital in place of labour in the production process there are also questions concerning the type of labour to use and how best to utilise it. Should there be one homogeneous grade of teacher for example, or should teachers and some type of assistants be used? Should classes be of more or less uniform sizes meeting for uniform periods, or should varying class sizes and time-periods be used depending on the subject matter?

The most usual form in which the question of labour utilisation arises in education concerns the size of class. Harris reviews the more recent evidence for the college level, all of which seems to show that size of class is not in itself a significant element in educational effectiveness. Thus a series of experiments in the 1920s, with classes ranging from 12 to 159 students, concluded that 'in the light of all of the available evidence, class size seems to be a relatively minor factor in educational efficiency measured in terms of student achievement . . . In 78 per cent of the experiments, a more or less decided advantage accrued to the paired students in the large sections, only in the remaining 22 per cent was there any advantage in favour of the smaller classes'.

A more recent survey of a large number of experiments in class size reached the following conclusions:

> (i) Under prevailing methods class size bears no significant relationship to educational efficiency as measured in terms either of student achievement or of any other measurable outcomes. (ii) The only other instructional procedures that have appreciably and certainly increased student accomplishment in small college classes are prohibitively expensive, and costly in time and labour to be used in large classes and are of doubtful justification in any size of class. (iii) Most of the advantages of the small classes and materialistic methods of instruction accrue to the weaker students. (iv) The only assured effect of frequent and intimate teacher-pupil contacts is personal satisfaction. (v) If pupil differentiation is a commendable aim it appears to be more obtainable in large classes. (vi) There is no evidence to show that, native ability equal, students learn less under modern college conditions than they did when classes were small, methods personal and relationships intimate.

In addition to variations in class sizes as such, it is also possible to alter the teaching inputs required by, for example, using assistants to take discussion groups, mark essays etc., or by altering the amount of formal lecturing or classes and replacing them by more independent study on the students' part. Harris again reviews the bulk of the experiments which have been undertaken in these fields and again the results though not yet conclusive are interesting, as they suggest that the same or better standards of student performance can be obtained by these methods. Once again then the inference is that longer-run cost-effectiveness studies would need to take account of these alternative production methods.

Finally, with respect to longer-run educational choices, two remaining questions which need to be posed are: first, the type of curricula which schools should offer; and, secondly, the ages at which education should take place. To some extent these questions may be considered as being interrelated since the content of a curriculum is in many cases affected by the age of the students. It is not proposed to embark on a discussion of such topics as the 'optimum' ages at which children should start school or be introduced to specific subjects since these more properly belong to the realm of educational research. Instead it is merely proposed to raise the broad implications which the developments of the recent past hold for cost-effectiveness analyses of educational systems.

The question of curriculum content and timing has been extensively debated in recent years. The reasons underlying this questioning of traditional curricula have been well summarised in a recent review of the problem which is worth quoting at some length.[7] Referring to the position of O.E.C.D. countries it states:

> Only a few generations ago, formal education was the privilege of a limited number. The language of instruction was predominantly Latin and the substance of education was largely dominated by languages, literature and moral philosophy—a heritage which in many countries is regarded today not merely as a major part, but the most esteemed part of scholarship. It was only comparatively recently that the mother tongue in most European countries replaced Latin, and that instruction in science and formal history was included in the curriculum. Moreover, religion was in most countries a more direct and influential force in the operation of schools and in the determination of what was taught. Education was dominated by the general theory that knowledge was 'encyclopaedic' in nature, that it accumulated with

[7] *Curriculum Improvement and Educational Development*, O.E.C.D., Paris 1966.

the passage of time, and hence, that scholarship was largely a process of mastering a universal body of essentially static and factual knowledge. The expansion of knowledge was accomplished largely as a process of deduction, that is a process of deriving new knowledge from the logical spinning-out and refinement of hypotheses and propositions. The revolutionary inductive method of intellectual enquiry took a long time to establish itself as the basis for the modern approach to research and learning.

The report then suggests three ways in which modern attitudes affect curricula:

> Perhaps the first (change) is the gradual shift from the conception of knowledge as an exploration of a relatively fixed encyclopaedia of universal knowledge . . . to the conception that knowledge is limitless and capable of indefinite expansion. The belief . . . has profound implications for both the substance and the methods of education. The second fundamental change is that education as a whole has come to have much greater concern with its role of social utility than was previously true . . . This fact has transformed education as an activity the effects of which were essentially socially restrictive, that is to limited numbers and the support of established institutions, into an instrument of social service from which an entire society may profit . . . A third basic change of education conception . . . [is] the increasing orientation of present day education towards the future rather than the past. As a result education is . . . becoming an instrument of power for bringing about social, political and economic changes, while still conserving all its traditional characteristics as a means for developing and transmitting the culture of the past. All of these developments . . . have accelerated with a speed which now makes the crowding of the curriculum, the selection of subjects and the organisation of knowledge major problems of education. Many of these problems reveal themselves

specifically in the evolution and adaptation of curricula in the member countries of O.E.C.D. today.[8]

The attitudes reflected in these extracts are indicative of the widespread dissatisfaction with which existing curricula of education institutions are viewed, and suggest that any comprehensive cost-effectiveness studies of education would call for the incorporation of curricula analyses into the total evaluation of the system. This in turn calls for an examination of the timing of education. The traditional approach has been to expose the pupil to a continuous period of anything from 8 to 18 years' education, after which education ceased and the pupil took up employment. In the contemporary situation it is increasingly recognised that such an educational preparation becomes obsolete in many occupations, with the result that many people require 'updating' or 'refresher' courses in order to keep abreast of new developments in knowledge. This would suggest that one further development might be to shorten the initial period of education and formally to incorporate periods of adult education into the design of educational systems. To allow for rapid changes in knowledge in this way it would, of course, be also necessary to take account of relative efficiency in the learning process itself. It may, for example, be necessary to devote some minimum period to each subject if it is to produce significant effects. Thus the report mentioned above, commenting on timetables for different countries, noted that 'a foreign language may, for example, be included in the curriculum, but if its study is not given sufficient time to achieve a fair degree of mastery, the time will have been largely wasted as language study, and will have been diverted from other subjects where it might have been more profitably spent'.[9] This suggests that the marginal hypothesis is not necessarily correct when considering the allocation of time both as between study and other uses and as between different forms of study itself, although the report added that 'nevertheless we must conclude that the number of hours per week

[8] *Ibid.*, 34-5.
[9] *Ibid.*, 36.

spent in school bears significant relation to the total educational achievement'.[10] Since little is known with certainty about the precise nature of the learning process itself, whether on the part of children or adults, it is again not possible to incorporate any precise information into a cost-effectiveness model, though it should be an important long-term objective to evaluate the outcomes of various learning arrangements.

III

The foregoing review of the various types of efficiency questions which arise with education, though brief, should nonetheless suffice to indicate the wide range of factors which are pertinent to any comprehensive assessment of the system as a whole. It is probable that many years will elapse before any full-scale assessment will be available, not only because of the large number of factors involved but also because the form of the relationship between many of the factors is unknown or uncertain. In the discussion each of the topics touched upon, such as the influence of school size, inputs or structure, or the level of attainment, the choice of production methods, or the selection of curricula, was largely considered in isolation. In practice they interact on one another, so that there can be a large number of possible combinations of elements used to produce any given educational attainment.

In particular, it should be apparent that any attempt to treat such aspects as the quality of education as being simply a function of the amount of resources provided, with more resources being equated to improved quality, is inadequate. Educational performance is a function of so many influences that the exploration of both quality and quantity changes can proceed in several dimensions. One recent model for the U.S., for example, designed for evaluating some programmes for the education of underprivileged groups, ran to 5 sub-sections, each of which had a minimum of 8 variables, even though it

---

[10]*Ibid.*, 37

was confined to a relatively limited set of influences in that the school system itself was taken as given.[11]

The almost total ignorance of efficiency aspects in education precludes any firm conclusions being drawn at this stage. Given this ignorance, however, it is highly improbable that existing educational systems are 'efficient' since it would only be by chance and not by design that they could be so. This suspicion of inefficiency is strengthened by the various pieces of circumstantial evidence which emerge from the studies quoted. Since education is now a major sector in so many countries, and accounts for such large expenditures, it seems certain that efficiency questions will receive growing attention in the coming years.

---

[11]C. Abt, *Design for an Education System Cost-Effectiveness Model*, O.E.C.D., Paris 1967.

CHAPTER 8

MIGRATION AND EDUCATION

THE earlier chapters have dealt with the main components in any general economic exploration of educational activity, and should lay the basis for an appreciation of the issues involved. A number of more specific aspects remain which are relevant to any comprehensive treatment of this subject. The present and succeeding chapter will be devoted to two of these specific aspects, namely, migration and finance, both of which can be of some importance at the practical level. Their practical significance, with obvious implications for influencing policy, demands that these two aspects be dealt with most carefully, given the danger that faulty policies may be derived from hasty or over-simplified analyses.

The present chapter deals with the question of migration and its relationships with education. This is an area which has aroused considerable interest and controversy in some countries. It has entered popular discussion as the 'brain drain' problem—the emigration of highly qualified personnel from some areas to others, mainly the United States. The 'brain drain' raises such questions as whether it is a good or bad thing, whether action should be taken to stop or alter the pattern of migration involved, or whether changes in educational policies are called for. Issues of this type are of some contemporary importance in a number or countries, and are undoubtedly of sufficient importance to justify an analysis of the relevant economic factors. It is not proposed, however, to present any comprehensive treatment of the subject here.

Apart from being confined to economics, the treatment which follows is further restricted in that it is solely concerned with migration insofar as it gives rise to educational consequences; it is not proposed to deal with the economics of migration in any general way.

The bulk of the economic literature relating to educational/ migrational links has concentrated on the permanent movement of those already educated from one area (city, state, country etc.) to another. Before proceeding to these aspects it may be useful to note that there is also some migration by people seeking education. Migration of this latter type arises at the higher levels of education, where the international movement of university students, for example, reaches significant proportions in many countries. The reasons why this is so, and why such migration (frequently temporary in nature) does not extend to education for the younger age-groups have in effect been discussed in chapter seven. On the demand side, population densities, coupled with the fact that a smaller proportion of an age-group go on to higher education, result in smaller absolute numbers of such students in any one area. On the supply side, the greater range of subjects and specialisations involved leads to larger universities (in terms of student numbers) than primary or secondary schools. In combination, these factors mean that universities will be comparatively few in number. To have access to any university will mean temporary migration for at least some section of the population. To have a choice of university would require that many more must move, since few centres would have more than one establishment. In addition, the greater cost of higher education means that the transport and other incidental expenses associated with migration will be of relatively less importance, and will constitute less of an obstacle to movement. Temporary migration may be seen as a rational method of obtaining or providing education for some sections of a population, and it is a method which is likely to be more relevant, the higher or more specialised is the type of education. This helps to explain, for example, why universities are frequently residential, but primary schools are not.

This statement needs to be qualified by noting that although the relative importance of migration may increase with educational level, its absolute amount need not (for example, 1 per cent of primary school students may represent a greater number than, say, 10 per cent of university students). The actual character of the migration associated with the lower levels of education may also be somewhat different, in that a family may change their residence within a given area, such as movement between suburbs of the same city in order to select particular schools for their children. Movements of this type would mean short-distance permanent migration in contrast to the longer-distance, but temporary migration which would characterise higher education.

The use of migration in providing education is more frequent within countries, than between countries. Reasons why this should be so are again not difficult to find. Apart from transport costs, which typically would be greater internationally than internally, cultural differences might make foreign courses less appropriate, and language differences would make them more difficult. In addition, where publicly-financed education is concerned, the absence of any ready-made machinery for inter-governmental transactions of this type may make governments reluctant to resort to international movement as a substitute for educational provision. Extending this last point in a somewhat different direction, it may be noted that in the absence of such machinery, international student movements give rise to a form of 'externality', in that the fees charged to foreign students generally do not equal the costs of providing their courses.

A brief but useful discussion of the main international flows of students in higher education is contained in the report on the Washington Conference of 1961, which dealt with the situation in member countries of O.E.C.D. in 1958/59.[1] In absolute terms, the U.S. had the largest proportion of foreign students, accounting for 38 per cent of the total in the member countries for which data were available; France and Germany were next with 14 and 12 per cent respectively, followed by the U.K. and Austria with 9 and 8 per cent. In aggregate these five countries accounted for 80 per cent of the 125,000 students involved. These absolute numbers accounted for very

[1]'International Flows of Students', *Policy Conference on Economic Growth and Investment in Education*, V, O.E.C.D., Paris 1962.

different proportions of the total student body in each country; thus the 47,000 foreign students in the U.S. constituted about 1½ per cent of the total student body. In contrast, the 10,000 who were in Austria constituted 32 per cent of the total student body in that country. In France they amounted to approximately 8 per cent, in Germany 9 per cent and in the U.K. 11 per cent of the total student body. About one-quarter of the total student flow represented movements between member countries of O.E.C.D. itself, 15 per cent came from Asia, 10 per cent from the Middle East and 7 per cent from Africa. While changes have occurred in the pattern of student movement over the past decade, the general tendencies displayed by this data still hold.

II

The more publicised aspect of migration, and the one which has received more treatment, is that of movement, usually considered to be of a permanent kind, by educated personnel. Migration, whether within or between countries, is not in itself a new phenomenon; much of this recent interest stems rather from the changes which have occurred in the characteristics of this migration. In the nineteenth century, for example, the flow of investment from Europe to the United States was accompanied by a large movement of people in the same direction. One study of these movements suggests that on the whole they benefited both the emigrant and the immigrant countries, and led to a narrowing of the differences in economic performance between the various areas.[2] In contrast, in a later article the same author suggests that while the importing countries still gain, the exporting countries may now be losing by migration;[3] a view which is shared by many writers on the subject.

Three main factors appear to account for these changed views on the consequences of migration; one is that a greater

[2] B. Thomas, *Migration and Economic Growth*, London 1954.
[3] B. Thomas, 'The International Circulation of Human Capital', *Minerva*, Summer 1967.

proportion of migration is now by highly qualified people, a second is that a much greater proportion of the cost of education of these migrants will have been met from public funds, and the third is that changes in immigration laws now tend to restrict inflows of unskilled labour and to favour the importation of highly qualified workers, in contrast to the greater freedom of movement in the nineteenth century.

Data on the educational or other qualifications of migrants are not available in any detail, but in recent years some studies have been made of movements by scientific and technical personnel, which may serve to illustrate the dimensions of contemporary migration. One such analysis, using data from two of the major sources—O.E.C.D. and the U.S. National Sciences Foundation—is that of Grubel and Scott.[4] This shows that over the 1949-61 period the inflow of scientific and engineering personnel from Europe to the U.S. was equivalent, in numerical terms, to about 5 per cent of the output in the same period from American universities. Measured in terms of American costs of production (teaching and other resources plus income forgone) these immigrants were valued at about $1 billion. Though not insignificant, these immigrants did not constitute a major change in U.S. stocks of such personnel. A somewhat different picture emerges however if these migrants are related to the position in the emigrant countries. Here the losses were distributed very unevenly. Expressed as a percentage of the output (graduates) of such personnel in each country for the period 1957-61, these emigrants ranged from 0·7 per cent for France to 22·4 per cent for Norway. Rather interestingly for the U.K.—a country where much reference to the 'brain-drain' has taken place—the figure was 9·9 per cent.

The study then goes on to examine whether the incidence of emigration among these professional groups differs significantly from that for the population as a whole, for clearly any inferences as to the losses or gains which might be expected from migration will differ between situations where professional movement differs markedly from general trends. For countries in which the relevant data were available it appears that professional migration was in fact relatively greater. In the Netherlands and Canada emigration to the U.S. by scientists and engineers was 12 times as great as for the population as a whole. For Sweden the ratio was 11 to 1, for Norway 10, for France and the U.K. 6, and Italy was the only country to record a low rate of 1·1 to 1.

In the case of the U.K., some evidence that emigration by personnel in these categories has been increasing in recent years is reviewed by Thomas in his recent study. In 1962, for example, the number of scientists and engineers admitted as immigrants to the U.S. was 665, which was very similar to the average for the 1956-61 period of 661, in 1963 the figure was 917, while for 1964 it had risen to 1,015.

The presence of greater migration rates among the more highly qualified personnel is in part to be expected for somewhat similar reasons to those listed above when discussing student flows. Transport and associated costs of movements would represent a smaller percentage of salaries for highly qualified people, and hence would constitute less of an obstacle to movement. Secondly, professionals are likely to possess a greater degree of information concerning job opportunities and other relevant factors than less qualified groups. There is also the probability that such personnel will speak more than one language, which would lessen one further obstacle to international movement.

The main economic effects produced by international migration are a redistribution of output and income as between countries. If the situations were such that all the conditions for a perfectly competitive market were satisfied, so that individuals captured all the benefits and met all of the costs associated with their activities, there would presumably be relatively little objection (at least of an economic nature) to migration, irrespective of whether the resulting redistribution of output and income took the form of a widening or narrowing of the gaps in average incomes per head between countries. This would be so, because individuals would be moving to the location which maximised their personal welfare, and in so doing, would not be imposing any hidden costs on others. Hence migrating could easily result in a greater concentration of high income people in one area and of a low income group in a second, as compared with some initial situation. While this would widen the gap in income per head between the two areas, it would still be the position which maximised both aggregate income and income per head for each group. This is because if any one person could gain by migration, then he would do so, hence the distribution of population which results from migration is that which is deemed to maximise each individual position.

Any economic objection to migration must therefore be based on the contention that the conditions for market perfection are not met. In practice the bulk of such objections are couched in the more specific form of suggesting that migration gives rise to externalities between the countries or areas concerned. The nature and consequences of such 'externalities' are matters which merit exploration in some detail.

One study directly concerned with these externalities—or to introduce the term which is frequently used for geographical effects of this type, 'spillovers', produced by the migration of educated people—is that of Weisbrod;[5] a study which has attracted comment from several quarters because of its rather controversial conclusions. The substance of Weisbrod's hypothesis is that with publicly-provided education (i.e. education for which the individual makes no direct payment), migration gives rise to spillovers because the costs of education are borne by the emigrant area, and the presence of such spillovers will lead to a level of educational provision that falls short of the social optimum. This will occur because any one authority will only extend the provision of education up to the point where the marginal benefits to its citizens equal the marginal costs to them, and will ignore any benefits which accrue to other areas. Weisbrod also argues that the shortfall from a social optimum would persist even where a community was receiving 'spillins' (or imports) of equal value to the 'spillouts' (or exports) which it was providing, because the

[5]B. A. Weisbrod, *External Benefits of Public Education*, Princeton 1964.

spillins of benefits to a community from education provided elsewhere would be largely independent of its own education expenditures. In effect the spillins constitute a type of lump-sum benefit which will have no influence on marginal decisions to raise or lower the amount of education provided within the area. This would imply that the tendency of spillouts to cause under-expenditure in education would not be offset by any tendency for spillins to cause over-expenditure, so that total spending on education would be likely to fall short of optimum. Weisbrod tests his hypothesis by undertaking a regression analysis between migration (as the independent variable) and public expenditure on education (as the dependent) for the different states in the U.S. The results showed a negative relationship between emigration and educational spending per person of school age, that is the higher the emigration rate the lower the level of education spending, and no relationship for immigration and educational spending. As such they were consistent with his hypothesis.

Criticism of this hypothesis and of the statistical result has come from several sources. The results were criticised by Malul, when reviewing the study, on two grounds.[6] One was that the study ignored private spending on education. If public provision was too low (for whatever reason), then when people became aware of the higher returns to education earned elsewhere they would themselves pay for education. Hence the relevant measure of educational spending should not exclude private expenditures. The second criticism was that Weisbrod had included federal government expenditures in his data on educational spending. These are unlikely to be directly affected by marginal calculations of the type posited by Weisbrod, and for his purposes state spending would have been the more relevant form of public expenditure to use.

A second criticism of Weisbrod's position is in a way an extension of Malul's first point. This comes from Holtmann who demonstrates that in a situation where communities seek to maximise their economic position, the individual (or his family) will pay the cost of his own education, in which case

[6]R. Malul, in *Journal of Political Economy*, December 1965.

migration by the educated will not give rise to external effects.[7] This conclusion is derived from a model which assumes first, that there are a large number of communities supplying and demanding education, so that any one community is a price taker; secondly, that all benefits of education are completely general and of value to all communities; and thirdly, that only communities can demand the services of educated people. Given these assumptions it follows that competition between communities will ensure that the price which communities pay for educated people will equal their benefit to the community. In these circumstances no community would provide free education, since people would emigrate if the community tried to recoup the costs of education by reducing the subsequent price it pays to individuals.

The second point raised by Holtmann was that Weisbrod had failed to distinguish the community's separate roles of producer and consumer and this led him to interpret the statistical data as support for his hypothesis. Holtmann suggests that it is equally possible that expenditures per pupil may reflect costs of providing education, whereas migration may reflect demand conditions for educated people. If this is so, the data could mean that those communities with low expenditures per pupil have a surplus of educated people relative to demand, whereas those experiencing shortages of personnel, and which consequently attract immigrants, have no distinguishing characteristics with respect to educational costs. Holtmann concludes:

> the major point is that one may imagine a whole host of reasons why the production of education may be non-optimal, but migration of people is not one of them. If the community is a net-benefit-maximising entity it will not produce education it cannot be reimbursed for. If it is not a net-benefit-maximising entity, the concept of optimal production and consumption becomes ambiguous.[8]

[7] A. G. Holtmann, 'A Note on Public Education and Spillovers through Migration', *Journal of Political Economy*, October 1966.
[8] *Ibid.*

A more general criticism of Weisbrod's position has been made by Williams.[9] This arises as part of a wider discussion of providing public goods in situations where their production gives rise to spillovers. The first point which Williams considers is the effect which spillins will have on the output decisions of a community. He demonstrates that where communities form expectations as to the amount of spillin which they will receive this will lead them to produce less of the good as compared with situations where no spillin is expected. Hence if output is below the optimum in Weisbrod's case (where spillins are ignored) it will be even more sub-optimal in those cases where spillins are taken into account.

This in turn raises the question as to what constitutes 'optimal' output, a question which Williams then discusses. On the assumption that a compensation scheme were established, whereby each community paid for any spillins which it received, and was itself paid for any spillouts which it provided to others, a pattern of income distribution between communities would be defined which corresponded to their initial production possibilities. The quantities of the publicly-provided, spillover-generating good, which the communities choose to produce in these circumstances could be defined as the status quo or non-redistribution optimum quantity, since their choice of output will take account of compensation payments and receipts. There is no reason to expect that the amount chosen in this status quo case will coincide with that selected in a situation where no compensation existed (and hence where spillouts would be disregarded). However, contrary to Weisbrod's conclusion, it is not possible to say whether the amount chosen in the 'no-compensation' situation will be greater than, or less than, the amount chosen in the compensation (optimal) position, since this will depend on the relative strengths which the changes in income and the opportunities for substituting other items for the relatively more expensive 'spillout' good will exert on the demand for that item. Williams points out that in addition, where spillins are expected by the communities,

[9]A. Williams, 'The Optimal Provision of Public Goods in a System of Local Government', *Journal of Political Economy*, February 1966.

the presumption that underprovision may occur in the aggregate is of course stronger . . . than in the Weisbrod case, because taking account of spillins always reduces output of the public good. But it is still possible to construct counter examples in which too much of the public good will be provided 'in the aggregate', but with the important qualification that it is *not* possible for each and every community to be oversupplied at the same time. If some communities have too much public good, at least one of the others must necessarily have too little, even though in the aggregate more is being supplied than is socially optimal.

While there is at least a measure of agreement among these various contributors in that they are each critical of Weisbrod's hypothesis regarding spillovers, the grounds for their criticisms differ widely. It is important therefore to clarify the issues involved.

Malul's points regarding the statistical data on procedures need not be discussed here, since they refer to the circumstances in one specific area; whereas the prime interest at this stage is with the general nature and validity of the analysis. The first point to consider is Holtmann's contention that educational spillovers in the form of migration would not in fact occur between economically-motivated communities. If this contention is correct it would simplify part of the analysis, because any spillovers which arose would then have to be attributed either to non-economic motivations (which would be outside the scope of this treatment) or to imperfections in the functioning of the market system.

It would appear, however, that this conclusion of Holtmann's is not as useful as it might seem at first sight, the reason being not that his analysis is defective but that it is too restricted. What he really demonstrates is that, in the conditions posited by him, the equilibrium position will be one where no 'migration' takes place between communities, and hence no such spillovers arise either.

The reason why this is so will be clarified by considering the situation in any community which is part of the competitive system described by Holtmann. In this world of competition between communities, the price paid for educated people will be the same in all areas. Or more precisely, the net benefits derived by the individuals concerned are the same since there might be differences in living costs between areas which would produce price differences. But this equality of price means that at the margin there is no incentive to migration, since the individual is equally well off in any area. Any migration which occurs must then refer to a disequilibrium situation, where the movement of people arises as part of the adjustment process designed to produce a new equilibrium.

An illustration of such an adjustment process would be the effects following some disturbance or change in circumstances. Initially, for example, it might be supposed that all communities were 'closed' ones in the sense that no movement of people between them could take place. Equilibrium in the demand and supply of educated people in such circumstances would be the result of purely domestic influences. If movement between the communities is then made possible, it would be expected that a redistribution of educated people would take place with migration from those areas of initial low-price wages to those with higher prices. This process would be expected to continue until prices in each area were brought into line with each other, at which point migration would cease.

Clearly once-for-all adjustments, such as this example, are not very helpful if the objective is to examine situations where migration is a continuing feature. For this we need demand and supply conditions in the various communities to be such that some are continuously attracting educated people from others. It is not impossible to envisage the existence of such situations, and since they will be ones in which individuals pay for their own education there is no reason to suppose that they would not be permitted to persist.

But one obvious query arises regarding the characteristics of such a position, namely that of optimality in educational supply. As noted above, Holtmann had concluded from his analysis that migration by educated people will not cause production of education to be non-optimal. However, he gives no indication as to how optimal output should be defined in circumstances of continuing migration. It has been seen that

Williams in his discussion had defined optimal output by reference to the position where compensation would be payable for spillovers but as he remarks, 'what is implied by all this is that "the social optimum" is defined with respect to the particular intercommunity distribution of purchasing power (real income) implied by the initial factor endowment. It is therefore a status quo or non-redistributive optimum'.[10] Clearly such a definition would not apply in a position where migration is a continuing feature, since migration means that the factor endowments, and hence the production and income characteristics of various communities, would change continually.

This means that Williams' analysis, contrary to his statements, does not directly deal with Weisbrod's case, since it is confined to final consumption items. Williams himself points this out as only one of several possibilities. There are cases where spillins take the form of inputs rather than the directly consumable services which he had been considering. It has been seen that migration (which Weisbrod discussed) involves a transfer of inputs. Williams' discussion would in this context only refer to pure 'educational' spillovers, that is to intercommunity transfers of 'disembodied' educational effects. It is possible that such spillovers occur and are important in their own right, but it is not proposed to explore such possibilities here, given that the prime focus of interest is on migration, whether with or without spillover effects.

Since Holtmann's model does not deal with situations in which migration actually occurs, it cannot be used to analyse the consequences for education produced by this migration. The Williams analysis, on the other hand, is helpful in that it demonstrates as a general proposition that in cases where final consumption items are involved, spillovers will not necessarily lead to the sub-optimal provision which Weisbrod has posited.

When it comes to explaining the consequences which migration might have for education in economically-motivated communications, however, it must be concluded that neither of these analyses permits a determination of the extent or even the direction which any such effect might take.

[10] *Ibid.*

G

III

Apart from the question of direct impacts on education, there is also that of the general economic consequences which result from the migration of highly educated personnel. This topic is one which has been explored by several authors and is of interest since the analyses frequently lead to statements of a policy-oriented kind.

One general discussion is Peston's treatment of spillovers in an educational context.[11] This takes as a starting point the existence of conditions which give rise to migration and spillovers, and then discusses whether or not any conclusions of either a positive or a normative nature can be derived from the existence of such spillovers. Using income per head as the measure of welfare, he suggests that the migration of educated people need not mean any reduction in the well-being of the remaining population. This could be so where migration was needed in order to avoid over-population, with education as the mechanism for promoting such migration. Again, it might be that relatively uniform education is provided by a community which results in shortages with some and surpluses in other categories of educated personnel. These imbalances might in turn be rectified both by emigration and immigration. It is equally possible that the contrary results might be obtained with migration leading to social costs. This might be especially so in cases where education is publicly provided in the expectation that it will give rise to social benefits within that area.

Having thus suggested that either a positive or negative outcome could result from migration Peston then, rather interestingly, goes on to refer briefly to migration from the U.K. Taking the costs of his education to be a debt owed by the emigrant, he suggests that a tax on migration might be appropriate, and states that there seems to be no good reason (other than difficulty of administration) why either physicians or teachers should not be asked to pay at least part of the costs of their education before migrating.

[11] M. Peston, 'Education and the Theory of Spillovers', *Public Finance*, March 1966.

A alternative solution for this type of situation is advanced by Goode, who suggested that geographical inequalities of income and wealth are likely to be increased because on balance the migration of the educated is from the poorer to the richer countries.[12] He goes on to reject the notion of restrictions on migration as a solution because of the reduction in individual freedom and the cultural losses which would be entailed. His proposal is that the richer (immigrant) countries should compensate the poorer (emigrant) ones for any educational spillovers which occur.

In contrast, Grubel and Scott suggest that emigration should be welcomed wherever the emigrant improves his own income by doing so, and when his departure does not reduce incomes for those remaining in the region of origin.[13] They advance several reasons why these conditions will generally be fulfilled in practice. One is that there is unlikely to be any cost imposed on the community by way of a loss in external benefits resulting from individual migration. The reasoning for this view is that even if significant externalities are produced by an individual in his initial occupation, these are not likely to disappear when he emigrates, but will probably continue to be produced by his successor. It would only be where the externalities are 'personally' linked with the individual that his movement would cause any permanent loss of this type. The more likely form of costs to the community which would result from emigration would be those of a short-run adjustment nature, such as the time and costs associated with finding or training a successor. On balance the authors feel that any such short-run costs are unlikely to be substantial, though they recognise that they would be of greater relative importance in the case of experienced professionals by comparison with, say, a newly-graduated student. Counterbalancing any such costs which may arise is the possibility that locating the individual in the new environment can result in beneficial spillover effects to his original community. The illustration given is that of immigration by scientists, leading to an increased fund of knowledge, much of

---

[12]R. Goode in *Financing of Education for Economic Growth*, O.E.C.D., Paris 1966.

[13]H. Grubel and A. Scott, 'The International Flow of Human Capital', *American Economic Review, Papers and Proceedings*, May 1966.

which may flow back free of charge to the scientists' countries of origin. Grubel and Scott conclude from their analysis that there are good grounds for continuing present policies, and for the free movement of human capital throughout the world.

Thomas, on the other hand, in his recent article quoted earlier, is critical of such conclusions, and suggests that they stem from an attempt to apply the type of reasoning appropriate in a fully-competitive model to a second-best situation characterised by various imperfections. Given the long time-periods needed to produce highly qualified personnel, it is possible that the short-run adjustments, noted by Grubel and Scott, may last for quite long periods. Again, it is not obvious that new knowledge produced by emigrating scientists will return free of charge. It is equally possible that such 'know how' may have to be bought, and here Thomas refers to estimates of the 'technological' balance of payments which showed that in 1961, for example, U.S. sales of 'know how' brought in $577 million, whereas their purchases from abroad amounted to $63 million. It would be a matter for research to establish how flows of free knowledge between countries compared with such commercial transactions.

A further point to which Thomas draws attention is that the migration flows which exist are not the product of relatively free choice, but can be highly influenced by immigration regulations. One example which he cites is the 1965 revision in U.S. immigration regulations, which abolished the earlier system of quotas for various nations and substituted a global annual total, within which applicants are given priority on the basis of their skills. The combined effect of these changes should apparently be both to increase the proportion of highly qualified personnel admitted, and also to raise the proportion of such personnel who come from the underdeveloped countries, because under the older system of national quotas European areas traditionally obtained the bulk of the total quota.

On the policy side Thomas concludes that only tentative suggestions are possible because of the incomplete nature of the available data. For the U.K. he suggests that there is a strong case for reducing marginal tax rates for the professional and executive income groups, for reviewing the methods of financing higher education and for providing higher salaries and increased opportunities for young people with high qualifications.

The range of views revealed by these various authors is an interesting example of the way in which similar analytical approaches can lead to diverse, and frequently conflicting, policy conclusions. The example is made more interesting by the fact that the policy statements are at best only partially substantiated by the respective analyses, and should consequently be treated with some caution.

Peston's suggestion, for example, that migrating physicians and teachers be asked to repay at least part of their educational costs raises a number of queries. The Grubel and Scott analysis suggests that the loss of experienced personnel is likely to be more costly than that of the newly-graduated. At the same time the former group will have been paying taxes on their earnings over the years since their graduation, so that if a tax is imposed on emigrants it is not clear whether experienced personnel should be required to pay the same, a larger, or a smaller amount than new graduates. A second point about Peston's suggestions is that if the tax is confined to doctors and teachers it may have the effect of reducing the numbers of students in these subjects. Peston does not state why a tax on these categories of emigrants would be appropriate, but possibly the intention is to stop the outflow of existing personnel, already in short supply. If this is the objective, the tax might improve the short-run position, but it could also aggravate the long-run situation if it led to a reduced future flow of students and graduates. This would imply that a tax on all graduates might be the more appropriate measure.

To decide whether a tax, of either a partial or general nature, on graduate emigrants was appropriate would require a more extended analysis than that presented by any of the authors. It would not be appropriate to embark on such an analysis here, but two points may be used to illustrate the problem. The first is to ask why the spillover of graduates is taking place; that is, why does the government subsidise university education in a situation of continuing graduate migration? Clearly there can be a variety of reasons involved, not all of which are likely to be of an economic character. Information is rarely available on

H

the precise characteristics or objectives of government expenditure, and in its absence it is not possible to decide unambiguously whether any particular spending is 'efficient' or not. The second point is that even for situations where only economic motivations and consequences are relevant, the effects of such spillovers should still be contrasted, not with some hypothetical model, but with the alternative situations which would be expected. In the case of the U.K., what is needed is some picture of the situation which would result from the impositions of the suggested tax. It may well be that this position would be better (economically) than the existing one; equally it is possible that it might not. Thus if the tax cuts down emigration the resulting increase in the domestic supply of graduates may lead to a decline in their relative salaries. This in turn, among other possible effects, might lead to a fall in the proportion of graduates among immigrants to Britain. Depending on the relative strength of each effect, it is possible that the loss entailed by having fewer such immigrants would outweigh the gain in reducing emigration by domestic graduates. Other possibilities exist also, but the illustration should suffice to suggest that the case for a tax be marked 'not proven'.

Similar remarks might apply to Thomas' suggestions for reducing tax rates, or providing higher salaries to graduate-type personnel. Given the extent to which remuneration in the U.K. appears to be influenced by 'equity' considerations (in terms of relativities between various occupations) and to be controlled by incomes policies or similar directives of a general nature, it is possible that the frictions generated by attempts to implement these proposals could produce costs greater than those associated with the existing migrational spillovers.

The suggestion by Grubel and Scott that the existing system of international movement be maintained is likewise open to doubt, since it follows on an analysis which was couched in terms of a predominantly competitive framework, whereas the existing system is characterised by various types of restrictions and obstacles to international migration. The nature and consequences of these restrictions vary as between countries so that no general summary of their impact can be presented. It seems reasonable to suggest that there is no evidence that this existing pattern represents the best position from either an international or individual viewpoint. As Thomas suggests, it may be to the advantage of some countries, but that is another question. The logic of their own analysis would imply that Grubel and Scott might more appropriately have recommended the abolition of existing restrictions on migration.

Finally, it may be noted that Goode, while airing laudable sentiments in suggesting that the immigrant countries might compensate the emigrant areas for the educational transfers involved, is likewise proposing something which does not follow from his own analysis. His basic theme is that it may be in the interests of the immigrant countries to subsidise education in the emigrant areas. This would, if the objective is one of economic efficiency, lead to a somewhat different policy, namely that it would pay some countries to draw their requirements of educated people from other low-cost producers of education, rather than expand or continue their own high-cost domestic output. This would be analogous to the normal free trade argument for the importation of some products, complicated, however, in this case by the fact that the required product (education) can only be imported jointly with a factor (the person). It thus raises the problem of defining optimality in educational provision and migration discussed earlier in this chapter. To the extent that poor countries are also the low-cost producers of education, this efficiency approach might approximate to Goode's proposal; it is most unlikely that it would be identical with it, since not all of the poorer emigrant countries would be likely to emerge as efficient low-cost educational producers. In fairness to Goode it should be added that he stressed the non-economic motivations underlying both existing policies and his own proposals, so that his economic analysis might be regarded not to constitute the foundation of his case, but to show that his proposals were not in conflict with economic factors.

The various analyses discussed above, while they are of considerable value in clarifying the issues raised by migration, and particularly in showing the relevance of migration to questions of educational policy, do not in themselves lead to any general policy conclusions. The temptation to make policy statements on the basis of such limited analyses is understandable, since policy decisions must continually be made, and the alternative to providing a partial economic analysis may be to have economic aspects excluded from the decision-making process. It is to be hoped that this rather unhappy position will quickly be remedied as more theoretical and empirical analyses of these migrational aspects become available.

CHAPTER 9

THE FINANCING OF EDUCATION

THE discussion to this point has avoided any specific reference to the financial aspects of education. It was convenient to postpone the question of finance because the adequacy of financial arrangements can only be assessed when the nature of the policies or objectives which they are designed to promote are known. The discussion in the earlier chapters provides a convenient framework against which the examination of financial topics may proceed.

If education were treated as an activity of purely personal concern, then students or their families might be expected to pay the costs of their own education. The exceptions might arise from philanthropic acts, in that various individuals or organisations (including governments) might give donations either to student(s) or to education establishments, in much the same way that the theatre, cinema, art, etc. are supported. Were this the case, the expectation would be that the bulk of such donations would go to producers (educational establishments) rather than to consumers (students) since the usual objective with such philanthropy is to foster or promote the activity itself and to stimulate the general level of interest in the activity, rather than to promote enjoyment of the activity by some particular individual(s).

A discussion of financing in such circumstances would be largely concerned with the adequate functioning of the financial market, as applied to education. The main topics of interest would probably be those arising in the case of potential students who did not themselves possess enough money to pay for their studies and who could well experience difficulties in borrowing the required funds, even though on any reasonable estimate, the education concerned would be a lucrative investment. Two of the major reasons why would-be borrowers might experience difficulty can be discerned. One is the risk element. Students would on average be young and hence would have poorer credit ratings than older settled persons. The second factor is the illiquidity element. Prospective lenders would be deterred by the fact that there was no transferable asset which could be seized in the event of non-repayment by the borrower, because the educational investment must of necessity be embodied in the student.

Public sector action in the sphere of educational financing would be one way of coping with these difficulties. If governments were to act as guarantors for student borrowing, this would presumably enable commercial lenders to advance funds to students on the same terms as those obtaining on first-class risks generally. This is not to imply that public sector action would be the sole method of dealing with these difficulties; changes in customs or in the legal system where necessary which would result in enforceable contracts of service should have a similar result. These would mean that employers would advance funds to students in return for which the latter would undertake to work for a specified time-period on stated terms. In this way lenders would have a reasonable prospect of being able to recoup their loans.

This thumbnail sketch will serve to demonstrate the theme that where education is regarded as a private individualised activity, a reasonable functioning market mechanism might be expected to operate with little or no public sector financing.

A different financial pattern arises if emphasis is placed on the community aspects of education. If the concern is with the economic benefits of education—the returns by way of higher incomes for the rest of the community—there would be scope for public sector financing both on the demand side, in encouraging potentially profitable students to enrol, and on the supply side, in subsidising those forms of education which yielded the largest social benefits. Certain problems would, however, arise with each of these methods.

Subsidies to selected educational activities would be expected to have the effect of increasing the demand for the courses in question, but there is no guarantee that the extra students so attracted are the ones who will yield the largest social benefits.

Potential students may be expected to differ both with respect to their 'abilities' (used here as an estimate of future economic potential) and their financial circumstances. Given that both characteristics are randomly distributed, the size of subsidy which will attract a sufficient number of extra students may also be expected to attract a group whose ability levels range from the highest down to the lowest acceptable, and therefore to exclude another group with a similar ability distribution. If the objective is to maximise the return to the community, it would be preferable to pay larger subsidies where necessary in order to attract those students who would contribute most to the community. This would suggest that aid to students would be more efficient than subsidies to suppliers.

However, aiding students raises separate difficulties. One would be that of obtaining adequate data on the potential performance of individuals, since it would be necessary to predict not only their academic performance, but also their subsequent economic contribution to the community. Assuming that these data problems are overcome, the second problem which arises is that of determining the size of subsidy for each student or category of student. The upper and lower limits to the size of any subsidy can be identified readily enough. The maximum subsidy would be the amount where it was just worthwhile to pay for the student(s) concerned—a larger sum would be better employed in a switch to some other category. The minimum subsidy is the smallest sum needed to induce the student(s) to embark on the relevant course of study—any lower offer would mean they would undertake some other activity. The actual sum agreed upon would in part depend on the information and bargaining power possessed by both sides. The student may likewise be assumed to be economically motivated and hence interested in obtaining the maximum subsidy. Since students will differ in their circumstances and expectations, varying figures would probably prove acceptable to each. But for an individual in any given ability group, once an actual figure is struck it would quickly be generalised for all within the group, since all other comparable students would then know that they were at least worth this amount and would consequently not settle for any lesser sum. In many respects the attempts to determine the relevant subsidy would be comparable to the process by which wage rates are determined, with students developing some form of collective machinery for bargaining with the official side.

The form of financial aid which would be expected in cases where the community interest in education is non-economic in nature would depend both on the type of education and on the nature of the objective(s) sought.

For the younger age groups where the specification of a period of compulsory education is now a world-wide objective, the normal financial concomitant is the abolition of all direct payments by the students themselves. The relevant government department or agency assumes responsiblity for the payment of teachers and other necessary resources. It is perhaps worth digressing slightly to note that such public financing of schools is frequently accompanied by public control or operation of their activities, so that teachers become in effect one category of civil servants. Although public financing and public operation frequently accompany one another there is no necessary reason for them to do so, since it would be perfectly feasible for the public sector to pay pupils' fees at privately owned and operated schools. Returning to our main theme of financing, it may also be observed that public sector financing on a universal basis is not a necessary concomitant of universal compulsory education. It would be quite feasible to specify a period of compulsory education and still to charge fees for the majority of pupils, the exceptions being those cases where payments would impose hardship.

For post-compulsory levels of education, a major form of social objective is the provision of adequate opportunities for all sections to participate. As the discussion of the earlier chapters has demonstrated there are various forms in which objectives of this type can be specified. If equality of opportunity is viewed in terms of providing comparable access to existing facilities, then the emphasis would most probably be on financial aid to students from low-income families to meet fees, travel costs and, less frequently, maintenance costs. This is readily recognisable as the conventional scholarship system. If equality is thought of as also embracing access to comparable facilities, public sector aid to educational establishments should be expected as a way of ensuring adequate provision of facilities in sub-standard areas—programmes of this type might again be accompanied by public ownership or operation of educational facilities. Again if equality is formulated in terms of equal attainment levels, this would once more be expected to lead to public sector aid to both students and schools, but this time the aim would be the provision of unequal facilities, by way of positive discrimination in favour of disadvantaged groups.

The foregoing outline is by no means an exhaustive catalogue of the possible financing forms which could be adopted for education. The intention has been to demonstrate that a number of financing methods can be used, and that the choice of method should depend on the objective(s) sought. Financing is a means of attaining some end, and is not an end in itself. Attempts to assess the adequacy of financing methods used in practice must therefore necessarily depend for their success on adequately identifying the objective(s) of any expenditure programme.

It is not proposed to attempt any such examination of actual financing methods here, since this would call for a major comparative survey far beyond the confines of a single chapter. Most of the elements outlined above appear in the financing pattern of each country, but the actual emphasis given to each mode of finance varies not only because of differences in objectives and in the priorities accorded to them, but also because of institutional and other structural differences. Accordingly, it is proposed to focus here on selected topics which are likely to be of general relevance in educational financing.

The general experience has been that the educational sector has expanded, in many cases fairly rapidly, during recent decades and further expansion is expected in the coming years. It has also been the common experience, though less universally valid, that the public sector proportion of the total has been growing, and appears likely to continue doing so. In some cases the financing of this growth has already given rise to budgetary difficulties for governments. Much discussion has, not surprisingly, been concerned with the scope for altering the balance of public/private financing while at the same time ensuring that the ability to attain specified objectives is not impaired. Various proposals have been advanced which would affect both the demand and supply patterns in several respects, and it will be useful to explain some of these suggestions in more detail.

One topic which has attracted considerable attention in both the U.S. and Europe has been the role which loan financing might play. Generally this question is raised in the context of financing higher education, but it would in principle apply to any post-compulsory type of education. The need for loan finance arises in areas where students must meet at least some of the costs of their education, and such self-financing is seen as an obstacle to low-income groups. There have been frequent suggestions that the proportion of higher costs to be met by the students themselves should be raised, both as a way of curbing the growth in demand and because of the evidence indicating that students subsequently benefit financially from the education. Were this to be done, there would be a corresponding rise in the need for loans. Since this question of loan financing touches on almost all the issues raised by financing methods it is relevant to explore it in some detail.

One of the most extensive discussions of loan financing in education is that by Harris, who not only reviews much of the other published material on the topic, but also presents the results of his own inquiries among economists.[1] A majority of these preferred the use of scholarships and/or loans, rather than subsidised fee levels at educational establishments. This preference was, in part, based on the view that selective aid related to student needs was more economical of public funds than universal subsidisation.

Within this general consensus of aiding students there was a wide range and diversity in the points raised for and against the use of loans. The main points advanced in favour of loans were, first, by making poorer students less dependent on scholarships a loan would enable them to back their own belief

[1]S. E. Harris, *Higher Education: Resources and Finance,* Maidenhead 1962, chapters 17-22.

in themselves, rather than rely on some selection board's assessment of their prospects. Secondly, the burden involved in a loan would serve to separate the serious from the casual students, and help to foster more responsible attitudes among students. Thirdly, self-financing could provide greater freedom of action to the student in such matters as changing course, since scholarship rules can be fairly inflexible in this respect. Fourthly, it might enable institutions to raise their fees and thus provide higher quality instruction. Fifthly, if loans were used it would enable higher education to obtain a larger part of total resources because part of the available credit facilities would be diverted from other fields—such as consumer durables—to education.

Arguments against loans also took several forms. One was that it would discriminate between students who would be forced to take loans and those who would not. A second was that loans would cause students to desert arts courses in favour of the more lucrative sciences and professions. A third point was that it would create a new class of long-term debtors who would have a vested interest in continuing inflation to enable them to shrug off their debt. A fourth was that by weakening the sense of obligation to their parents for providing education, it would weaken family ties, and specifically would lead to more demand for government support of the aged. A fifth was that it ignores the fact that society as well as the individual benefits from education.

At the more practical level several other factors would be needed to make extensive loan financing feasible. One would be the necessity for some form of official guarantee or insurance scheme, especially if the intention was to attract private capital into this field. Guarantees would also be needed to persuade students to use this form of finance; while on average the returns to education might be high, it would still be possible for any one individual to show no profit on his spending. It would also be necessary to ensure uniformity of credit arrangements between different institutions and courses, otherwise some students might be choosing their studies, not on any educational grounds, but rather on the basis of who was offering the best credit terms.

In the subsequent discussion Harris considers these and other contributions to the debate, and refers to other points of interest, for example, the special problem of girls who borrow and then subsequently marry, and whose loan commitments might then constitute a form of 'negative dowry'. On balance Harris argues the need for loans, not necessarily to cover the total cost of education, but at least that part which will be reflected in private returns. Subsidising would then be restricted to that part of education which provides social benefits. On this basis he suggests that a loan scheme with an interest rate of 4 per cent and repayable over forty years would be a practical proposition, which would ease the burden of official financing, and yet not impose undue strain on the borrower, especially if, as Harris assumes, real incomes continue to grow in the future, so that repayments constitute a declining proportion of income.

However, at the level of practical schemes it may be more interesting to consider Vickrey's suggestions, which are more fully articulated than those of Harris.[2] Vickrey, like Harris, considers that there is scope for loans, not to supplant but to supplement other forms of finance, and in his view the main drawbacks to be surmounted before loans are viable are: first, that the students' fear of inability to repay must be overcome; secondly, that any stigma of loans being a form of charity (e.g. because of subsidised interest rates) should be removed; and thirdly, the necessity to provide funds on a scale large enough for students to obtain sufficient financial support. The scheme which Vickrey proposes uses a 'combination of the techniques of mutual investment, the limited dividend corporation, pension funds and income taxation' so that arrangements can be devised which will promise reasonable returns and security to the investor, while at the same time offering the student terms that he can readily accept.[3]

The substance of Vickrey's scheme is that students would be able to borrow fairly liberally, to cover not only their immediate tuition costs, but also any earnings forgone. Repay-

[2]W. Vickrey, 'A Proposal for Student Loans', in *Economics of Higher Education*, Washington 1962.
[3]*Ibid.*, 269-70.

ment would be made later, not on any fixed interest plus amortisation basis, but in the form of a dividend on the higher earnings made possible by education. Students who did not achieve higher earnings would make no repayment. The actual values to be used would be on an average basis, and could be revised in the light of changing circumstances and experience. As an illustration it might be supposed that high school graduates earn an average of $4,000 annually. A student who borrows for a college degree would then be exempt on the first $4,000 of subsequent annual income, but might pay $\frac{1}{2}$ per cent on the next $1,000, 1 per cent of the second $1,000, and $1\frac{1}{2}$ per cent of all income in excess of $6,000, for every $1,000 which had been borrowed. Thus a student who subsequently earns $8,000, and who had borrowed $3,000 ,would be paying $135 each year ($15 on the first eligible $1,000, $30 on the second, and $90 on the remaining $2,000, the actual amounts in this case being three times those payable on a $1,000 loan).

Vickrey's other suggestions are designed to cope with some possible objections to a scheme of this type. One such objection is that if students' subsequent earnings exceed expectations they may be repaying 'excessive' amounts. The mutual-fund principle is suggested as a means of overcoming this. Briefly the idea would be that interest on invested funds could first be set at some minimum level, say 5 per cent. Beyond this point earnings from dividend repayments could be allocated in part to the investors until interest reached some maximum level such as 7 per cent. The remainder would then go to an account for the borrowers. From this latter the borrowers might be able to draw retirement benefits in their later years. A second difficulty to be overcome would be that of adverse selection. If applicants were not carefully screened there would tend to be a greater proportion of requests from students who felt that their future income prospects were below average, and hence would have little or no repayments to make. In contrast, students with high income expectations would be more reluctant to commit themselves for what could amount to a substantial portion of their income. Accordingly it would be necessary to adopt the insurance approach of rating the risk in each instance. This could be done by using data on educational attainment, test scores, etc. When the student applies, an assessment would be made of his earnings potential, both with and without the proposed course. The loan would then be made on this assessment. This would mean that a student with a low earnings potential would be given a low exemption limit, hence he would have less chance of avoiding repayment, whereas the student with higher income potential would have a higher exemption limit. This should also mean that the lower potential students would be less likely to apply, unless they had some reason to expect that their future incomes would rise by a worthwhile amount. Finally, it would be necessary to co-ordinate all dividend repayments with income tax assessments, otherwise it might be possible for combined tax and dividend payments to approach 100 per cent of marginal increments of income, and thus constitute a serious disincentive effect. The suggested solution to this would be to make the dividend repayments a deduction in computing net income for tax purposes. This could be done even on the strictest interpretation of (U.S.) tax rules, by treating the original loan as income for tax purposes (when presumably it would be subject to little or no tax), in which case the subsequent repayments would have to be treated as a deductible expense in order to avoid double taxation.

Vickrey concludes by suggesting that some such type of loan financing may be desirable not only as a means of enabling universities to raise their fee levels, but also as a way of preserving the independence of private institutions, which otherwise might become increasingly dependent on state support. Vickrey also recognises that loan financing would be extended to state colleges on the basis of an equity argument, in that an individual whose earning power had been improved by public spending could be regarded as owing an extra amount of financial support to the state by comparison with others who had reached the same income level by their own efforts. Such greater financial support would be achieved if students were asked subsequently to repay the costs of their education.

Before considering these views it may be of interest to refer to the comments of two British writers on the topic. The first of these by Lees, appeared in the same volume as Vickrey's proposals.[4] Lees supports the notion of loans as being applicable in British circumstances also. His main reason for doing so is the same as one of Vickrey's arguments, namely that it would ensure the independence of the universities. The chain of reasoning in support of this view is as follows: in the U.K. the system of student grants means that the fee income of the universities largely originates from government sources and the bulk of non-fee income is by way of direct government grants to the universities, so that there is a high dependence on government funds. A system of self-financing by students would sharply reduce this dependence. Lees continues that this reason for advocating loans may well be unique to Britain, but it reinforces the more orthodox arguments based on the personal gain which education produces.

The second British author is Prest, who has discussed educational financing in the context of both the U.K. and developing countries. In his discussion of university financing in the U.K., Prest reviews the various possibilities and opts for a loan system which would operate along lines very similar to those put forward by Vickrey.[5] In addition to the pros and cons listed by the other authors, Prest also considers one further problem which is of relevance in British circumstances, namely, emigration by graduates. If a loan scheme were operating it would clearly be difficult to collect repayments from those living abroad, although Prest points to the Dutch practice of using their embassies to contact non-payers. A further possibility would be to demand a lump sum from the emigrant before he leaves the country. Would-be emigrants might not themselves always pay this sum since many leave to take up specific appointments abroad, and their new employers might well pay such sums if they needed the personnel badly enough.

Although Prest is an advocate of loans in developed countries, he feels that there are several objections to them in the case of developing countries.[6] One reason is that the equity argument

---

[4]D. S. Lees, 'Financing Higher Education in the U.S. and Great Britain', in *Economics of Higher Education*, Washington 1962.

[5]A. R. Prest, *Financing University Education*, Institute of Economic Affairs, Occasional Paper No. 12, London 1966.

[6]A. R. Prest in *Financing of Education for Economic Growth*, O.E.C.D., Paris 1966.

for grants as redistributing income is weaker, because there are far fewer university students in these countries. A second is that the administrative machinery for tax collection is seldom sufficiently developed to be able to cope with this extra complication in the tax structure. A third reason is that many university students in these countries study abroad, and the introduction of liability for repayment of educational costs would reduce the incentive to return home when their studies were completed.

These various treatments of loan financing serve to illustrate the range of issues which this form of finance raise. It would seem that there are four main aspects to the discussion, the equity component, the efficiency argument, the independence issue and the practical aspects.

The independence issue can be disposed of quickly, because it is not an economic question, but rather one about the distribution of power in society, and hence is more appropriately left to political scientists. It may be noted, however, that where universities or similar institutions possess complete autonomy, they in turn normally enjoy a significant degree of economic power, because they occupy monopolistic positions in the supply of such education. It would therefore be necessary, on economic grounds, to explore either the ways in which comparable countervailing power could be developed for the consumers (students) in such situations, or other safeguards introduced for their protection.

Again, on the political power issue raised by Vickrey and Lees, it may be noted that the available evidence does not appear to indicate that public financing has led to any significant loss of autonomy by the U.K. universities. Bowen, for example, in comparing the U.S. and U.K. research positions concludes that although the British universities may obtain relatively smaller funds per person (which constitutes one form of constraint on behaviour), there are probably fewer inducements or pressures on their personnel to pursue particular lines of research than those existing in American situations.[7]

[7]W. G. Bowen, 'University Finance in Britain and the United States', *Public Finance* No. 1, 1963.

The efficiency aspect can also be more complex than would appear at first sight. The formal argument is straightforward. Individual(s) should allocate expenditures so that the satisfaction from the last unit of spending is equal in all uses. Similarly, a community should spend so that the marginal returns to it are comparable on all expenditures. Where both individuals and the community are sharing the cost, they should spend up to the point where the returns on the last unit of spending yield benefits of the necessary order to each party. In these circumstances the total amount spent on education will be influenced by the way in which the costs are shared between them. If both parties possessed adequate information and behaved rationally an 'efficient' solution could be expected. In practice, however, it is possible for anomalies to exist. It was seen in chapter two, for example, that individuals would tend to have stronger preferences for present rather than future consumption than would the community as a whole, and that in turn working-class people have stronger preferences than middle-class groups. This would suggest first that for any given mixture of public/private financing, a greater proportion of middle-class students would be expected, and secondly, that many potential students might not buy education, even though the returns to be expected might well be large enough to make further community spending on them attractive.

The problem here is that it would be necessary to have differential financing arrangements, tailored to the characteristics of each group, before a fully efficient pattern could be achieved. In practice the necessary degree of selective discrimination could not be achieved, but it is possible that a system with some differential components would be just as efficient as one without them. To explore this possibility more fully it would be first necessary to articulate the objectives desired. This will not be attempted here, but following on the discussion of earlier chapters, it should be apparent that for different objectives there would be different systems of 'efficient' financing.

A similar conclusion would hold for the equity argument, which is perhaps the main plank in the case advanced for loans. Because higher education leads on average to higher incomes, it is contended that community financing of education is in effect transferring money to a high income group, and is thus inequitable. In contrast, self-financing, with loans available for the impecunious would avoid this.

This equity argument is acceptable if applied to students as a whole versus the rest of the community. It is also possible, however, that there may be an interest in 'equity' as between groups of students. If there are non-economic goals, such as redistributing opportunities to earn higher incomes, it would be necessary to think of 'equity' in terms of equal treatment for those in equal circumstances but of unequal treatment for different groups, e.g. all 'poor' should all be treated on the same basis. A different basis, but one which would again apply to all within the group, would be adopted for the 'wealthy'. For example this pattern of intra-group equality, and inter-group difference, is the way in which 'equality' of treatment would be thought of when applying a progressive tax.

The Vickrey/Prest proposals for loan repayments to be based on subsequent income are particularly weak if any form of redistribution cum equality of opportunity is envisaged. The discussion in earlier chapters indicates that students from poorer backgrounds need a greater provision of educational facilities if they are to reach the same attainment level as their wealthier counterparts, or to say the same thing differently, they would record poorer performances if given equal facilities. This would imply that with the Vickrey/Prest schemes, students from poorer backgrounds would have lower potential income ratings, and would consequently start to make loan repayments at lower income levels. In other words, the greater the initial handicaps with which a student starts, the more he would have to repay if he succeeds in overcoming these handicaps. As such this scheme would be the one most likely to perpetuate the 'status quo' since it reduces the likelihood of students from poorer social groups achieving high net income levels in later life. It would only be in a very restricted sense, therefore, that full self-financing, incorporating loans would be the most 'equitable' system.

At the same time there is no particular reason for reverting to the other extreme and advocating community financing for all students, since on equity grounds one would not wish to subsidise wealthy students. This would suggest that a mixture of grants (for poorer) and self-financing (for wealthier) of students would be more appropriate on 'equity' grounds, the actual proportions of the two elements varying for each category of student.

Such a mixed grant/self-financing system would also be one feasible solution to another problem, the fourth and final issue to be dealt with, which is the practical one. Given that existing financing systems for higher levels of education are imposing strains on public finances, a movement towards a greater element of self-financing appears both necessary and feasible (since income levels are rising, enabling more private funds to be spent on education). This discussion has been concerned with the general arguments for and against a shift towards greater self-financing; the actual extent of such movement must in the final analysis be related to the circumstances of each community, so that the combination of public and private financing will reflect both theoretical intentions and practical limitations.

In the realm of publicly financed and operated education (typically compulsory education, but often extending to higher levels also), a different proposal, which has attracted considerable attention in recent years, is that for a 'voucher scheme' under which parents would be given a specified sum to be spent only on education, but which could be used by them for either public or private schools.[8] Some of the reasons advanced in favour of these vouchers are similar to those associated with loans. The point of departure is the general financing problem of the public sector to find the continually growing funds needed for the operation of its schools. At the same time many parents might be prepared to make some extra contributions towards meeting these greater requirements but are largely prevented from doing so, under existing systems, where the only alternative to the publicly-provided school is the private fee-

<hr>

[8]In the U.K. recent interest in this proposal stems from the suggestions of A. Peacock and J. Wiseman in *Education for Democrats,* Institute of Economic Affairs, Hobart Paper No. 25, London 1964. There is an extensive discussion in *Education: a Framework for Choice,* Institute of Economic Affairs, London 1967.

charging establishment. The choice is thus either to pay once, through taxation for the public school, or to pay twice, through taxation plus fees, for private schooling. In contrast, a voucher scheme would give each parent an amount equal to the average cost per pupil in the public school. Both public and private schools would charge fees, and parental preferences could then decide the pattern for private schools. If parents wanted more than the basic level of facilities they would supplement the voucher by payments of their own, and private schools would find that they could attract pupils by offering these extra services at higher levels. If, on the other hand, parents were satisfied with the basic level, private schools would find it necessary to keep fees down to the same level as those of state schools. The voucher scheme would thus provide a mechanism for establishing whether, and to what extent, parents wished to have more resources allocated to education. These extra resources would moreover come from private spending, so that there would be no extra burden on the state budget. It is contended that this system would also be more 'equitable' in that parents choosing private schools would not have to pay twice, for both public and private schools, but would have their extra spending, if any, confined to the difference in fee levels between the two forms of school. In addition there would also be a greater degree of effective freedom of choice under this system since the costs of opting out of the state system would no longer constitute such a barrier.

There are also various problems which could arise with a voucher scheme. One is that competition between schools may in some circumstances lead to increased costs per pupil. This would happen in cases where population densities were low, and the total number of pupils available not great enough to support more than one school of optimum size. Since a minimum number of teachers (and other facilities) are needed to ensure adequate courses, introducing extra schools would lead to a rise in the numbers of teachers, etc., needed to cater for the available number of pupils.

It is not clear what consequences would follow under a voucher scheme from such competition for limited pupil vouchers. If it occurred on a widespread basis, the average level of fees in private schools would be higher than the *initial* value of the voucher. If the value of the voucher were not increased, parents would eventually discover that the extra amounts which they were paying were not buying any better quality education, but were merely going to meet the higher pupil costs of small schools. However, pupil costs in the state schools would also rise when some pupils switched to private schools. If rises in pupil cost are used as the basis for raising the value of the vouchers themselves, then parents choosing private schools could find the value of their vouchers was rising by an amount equal to, greater than, or less than, the growth in fee levels, depending on the cost characteristics of the two types of school, and on the proportions of pupils opting for each type. The long-run outcome of such a system could thus be a blend of private/public schools, of comparatively small size and high cost per pupil.

A voucher system could also give rise to difficulties in attempting to provide 'equality of opportunity'. If vouchers of equal value are given to all parents, it would on balance be the higher income groups who would supplement these, and send their children to higher-cost private schools. This would produce an inverse situation to one of 'positive discrimination' in favour of disadvantaged groups. Several suggestions have been advanced to offset this tendency. One possibility is that vouchers of varying value would be given to those in different income groups, or with different numbers of children. A variable voucher system of this sort would of course call for a more elaborate administrative machine. A second possibility would be to give vouchers of equal value for all children but to regard them as income which would then be liable for income tax where appropriate. This would mean that the net amount available to the parent would fall as total income rose.

While then, there are wrinkles which would need to be ironed out, a voucher system in some form is one potentially feasible method of attracting more spending on education, without placing any additional burden on state budgets.

The discussion to date has focussed on items such as loans or vouchers, which are concerned with the balance between private and public financing of education. A separate area of interest is the manner in which any given pattern of public or private financing affects activities within a particular area of education.

One illustration of this latter problem is provided by the policies of universities with regard to fee levels for various courses. In practice the fees charged do not appear to reflect any economic objective, in that they do not vary with the costs of providing each course, nor do they relate to any apparent non-economic objectives. Harris, for example, quotes one university where the cost per student in the medical school was fifty-five times as great as that for training a student in the business school, but the difference in the fees charged was only a small fraction of this.[9] Similarly, for Harvard, courses in public health were costing eight times as much per student as those in law, but the law students were paying fees almost 20 per cent higher than public health students. It would be easy to extend the examples to show that fees are not based on the costs of providing courses. The serious lack of data on individual course costs is itself an adequate demonstration of this, since the absence of cost information precludes any possibility of fixing fees in this way. Nor do fees relate to the returns which students receive in later life. Harris points out that medicine and law are two of the most profitable courses from a private viewpoint, so that charging on the basis of returns would place these at the top of the fee scale. The same remarks would equally apply in many European countries. It is possible that the subsidisation of high-cost courses would be justifiable on economic grounds, if these courses gave rise to substantial indirect benefits to the community. Again, however, the absence of data rules out this possibility on practical grounds, and there are no obvious theoretical reasons for expecting the high-cost courses (typically professional and scientific) to confer greater indirect benefits than low-cost courses.

In cases where education is financed by a mixture of central and local government funds other problems may arise. Eide,

---

[9]Harris, *op. cit.*, 48-9 and 102-3.

for example, notes that in the Norwegian system, where up to 85 per cent of teachers' salaries for compulsory education may be met by the central government (the average figure was 60 per cent) there is a tendency for an unselective increase in teacher usage to take place, with the wealthier localities providing more and smaller classes than their poorer counterparts.[10] He also suggests that by carrying almost the full cost of teachers in the poor areas, where the system tends to be most costly (because of low pupil numbers), the central government has removed any financial pressure on these local areas to economise in their use of educational resources. This latter point about the way in which administrative rules may shape the use of resources in a publicly-financed system is one which would apply with equal force to many countries.

These examples, though brief, many serve as sufficient illustrations that the financing methods actually used are not neutral, but produce effects of their own on the pattern of resource allocation in education. Almost invariably these effects are glossed over in general discussions which regard financing methods as a minor administrative problem insofar as the supply side of education is concerned. One may agree with Eide's conclusion that 'existing forms of financial aid are often the expression of a static accountancy-minded way of looking at educational policy'.[11]

Finally, before concluding this chapter it will be useful to look at some of the wider aspects of financing policy which impinge on education. One of these is the operation of the general tax system, capable of producing biasses both for and against education. A discussion by Goode, relating to the operation of the income tax system in the U.S., points out that income tax discriminates against persons whose earned income partly represents a return on capital previously invested in education by comparison with persons who have invested little in preparation for their occupations.[12] This discrimination arises because educational costs cannot be written off

[10]K. Eide in *Financing Education for Economic Growth*, O.E.C.D., Paris 1966.
[11]*Ibid.*, 193.
[12]R. A. Goode, 'Educational Expenditures and the Income Tax', in *Economics of Higher Education*, Washington 1962.

against subsequent income in the same way as investment in physical capital is amortised. On the other hand any expenses necessary to maintain professional skill or knowledge are deductible, and this results in some interesting anomalies.

A doctor, wishing to specialise and who takes graduate courses in pediatrics, for example, cannot deduct the cost of these for tax purposes, whereas a second doctor who takes a short course reviewing several specialised fields, including pediatrics, 'for the purpose of carrying on his general practice' is entitled to a deduction. Goode suggests that the cost of any education designed to raise earning power should be allowed as a charge against taxable income. This would exclude any education of a purely consumption nature, and Goode is conscious of the difficulty in distinguishing the two components. He suggests that some working rules could nonetheless be formulated which would at least be an improvement on the existing position. For example, he suggests that elementary education has little economic motivation and consequently need not be allowed as an expense for income tax purposes. At other levels the proportions to be capitalised might range as follows: 100 per cent for professional schools, post-graduate courses and vocational training, 75 per cent for general college and university studies, and 25 per cent for high school courses.

Goode feels that the side effects of this change would not be pronounced in the educational sphere, though it should encourage colleges to raise their fees somewhat. In this respect the plan would tend to stimulate enrolments at private institutions, where charges are higher as compared with public ones. The effect on educational and occupational choices, however, is expected to be slight because forgone earnings are the largest part of personal costs and these, of course, would not be chargeable. One other benefit of such a scheme is that it would not discriminate between types of students; whereas the present system, under which the parents of children may claim an allowance for those who are in full-time education after the period of compulsory schooling, discriminates against poorer parents, who may not have a large enough income to derive any benefit from the concession.

Apart from these effects which the operation of the tax

system may have on education, there are other possible ways in which the general monetary and tax system can impinge on the financing and operation of education. One example is the way in which inflationary situations may influence education. However, it is not proposed to discuss more specialised economic topics of this type at this juncture.

The general conclusion from the discussion of this chapter is that, in their several ways, financing methods influence both the volume and composition of educational activity. In some cases the effects may be small, in others substantial, only rarely will it be the case that financing methods are neutral in their effects. An examination of the consequences of financing is thus a useful reminder of the subtle and complex interactions which can exist between the ends sought and the means selected for their attainment.

CHAPTER 10

THE RELEVANCE OF ECONOMICS TO EDUCATION

THERE are two aspects arising from the discussion on the application of economic concepts to education which are worthy of brief comment by way of conclusion. The first of these is the necessity of integrating the various strands of the analysis when dealing with an actual situation, the second is the relevance of an economic approach to actual educational questions.

For purposes of exposition, the various facets of the economic treatment of education were discussed in isolation. Thus in exploring the rate-of-return approach in chapter three or manpower aspects in chapter six, no attention was paid to the effects which migration might have on the outcome, and yet the discussion of migration in chapter eight suggests that these effects would be of importance in practice. It would be necessary therefore to incorporate these (and other) relevant elements into any appraisal of an actual situation.

In the case of manpower calculations, migration could be dealt with by extending the number of sectors, so that account would be taken of the inflows and outflows of people. In practice, of course, it is not easy to develop reliable projections of emigration by various categories of personnel, but this position will improve as information on the educational and skill levels of the population improves.

In principle, too, migratory movements can be taken into account in the preparation of rate-of-return calculations by incorporating the relevant data for the groups and countries affected. In these cases it would be interesting to see the extent to which rates-of-return, both to individuals and to society, were affected by migration. In particular it would be valuable to see whether patterns of migration for various educational groups showed any systematic relationship with rates-of-return in different areas.

For the latter purpose care would be needed in the interpretation of the data, because a high rate-of-return to education in a low income country might represent a smaller absolute sum of money than would a low rate-of-return in a high-income area. To decide whether migration is profitable or not, it would be necessary to calculate the rate-of-return which the income levels obtainable in the various areas would constitute in relation to actual educational costs in the specified country.

Given then that the necessary extensions to the analysis can be made, the remaining issue is that of the relevance or usefulness of economic analyses to educational questions. The immediate response to this question by many people would be that there exists none, a view influenced by a feeling that there is something dehumanising in analysing education by the same methods as would be applied to the production of ships and sealing-wax. It is easy to understand and sympathise with such a view; at the same time it must be observed that such sentiments, though laudable, are also unrealistic. No society has yet approached, let alone attained, a level of affluence where it can fully cater for all the demands of its members; so the problem remains of choosing how to best use its relatively scarce resources. Moreover, even if material goods and services were eventually to become abundant, the problem of choice would still be an important one for activities such as education, which demand a considerable amount of time from the consumer (the student in this case). Given that life is short, there would still be the problem of allocating time to best advantage, and this would call for a continuing economic-type analysis of the educational process. There is a necessity, then, to make economic-type choices in education: to decide how much and what types of education will be available; to decide who will obtain this education; what methods will be used in the educational system; and how the costs of providing this education are to be met.

The answers to these questions will not be supplied, although they may be affected, by non-economic statements. Agencies such as the United Nations may be warmly applauded for declaring that everybody has rights to education, but the sad reality is that such rights are inoperable in many parts of the globe, because countries are simply too poor to provide sufficient teachers, schools and other resources. Again, teacher groups may campaign for substantial cuts in the number of pupils per teacher, and point out that such a step would be desirable on educational grounds, but governments or parents or whoever is paying the bill may have to turn down such requests on the grounds of cost.

Education, in common with all other activities which use scarce resources, must be analysed and placed in the overall perspective of a community's limited resources on one hand, and its diversity of aspirations on the other. To do this satisfactorily it is necessary to possess adequate information on educational methods, and the costs associated with these, and also to have an adequate formulation of educational objectives. The various chapters have illustrated the methods by which these steps may be carried out. The description and analysis of possible objectives was, however, artificial in that economic objectives were examined in isolation from social or other educational goals. This division was adopted because of its convenience for exposition. In practice it would be necessary to specify objectives so that they take account of both economic and non-economic aspects. While this would render the analysis more complex, it is possible to make the necessary extensions, in the majority of cases. One way of doing this is to select one element in the total set of objectives as the one to be maximised, and to treat the remaining elements as constraints, that is as items which must meet some prescribed values.

The rate-of-return data for the U.S. quoted in chapter three can be used to illustrate this method, using the white/ negro groups. If the objective was the single economic one of maximising the returns from educational spending then the data would indicate that whites should be selected to fill any extra college places, because on average they recorded the higher rate-of-return. If, however, it was desired to have education of negroes incorporated as an objective alongside the economic one, this could be done in either of two ways, the choice between the two depending on the relative importance attached to each. If priority is given to the social objective the specification might read: maximise the return from college education, subject to the constraint that x thousand (or y per cent) of the places are to be allocated to negroes. Alternatively the specification might be: maximise the number of negroes attending college, subject to the constraint that the rate-of-return for any graduate (white or negro) does not fall below z per cent.

In the first formulation once the specified number of places have been set aside, any further negro applicants would compete with whites for the remaining places, and these would go to whichever students had the better income prospects (which on the basis of the data used would suggest predominantly white students). In the second formulation there would be no reserved places for negroes, but every negro applicant whose income prospects were adequate to meet the specified minimum rate-of-return would be admitted on a priority basis. The proportion of negroes actually admitted could range anywhere between zero and 100 per cent, depending on the relationship between the specified minimum return and income prospects for negroes.

Other variations of these formulations could be suggested, but the examples given should serve to illustrate how multiple interests can be incorporated into an operational objective. It will be observed that this type of formulation is a method of coping with the problem of the interaction between ends and means, exemplified by the financing discussion of chapter nine. Thus in terms of our negro/white example it might be that the ultimate aim is to raise income levels of negroes, and that social welfare payments might be the most efficient way of doing this. If, however, it is decided that it is preferable for people to earn these higher incomes for themselves, then the educational programme may have been selected as the best means of achieving this goal of higher earned income.

It is possible, then, to articulate useful and relevant goals for educational activities which can be based on, and evaluated by, systematic analyses. Although there are still many areas where further theoretical development would be required before a fully adequate system resulted, the major deficiency hindering the application of existing concepts is that of inadequate data. Whether the interest is in the economic or other objectives of education, there is widespread ignorance on the actual operation and consequences of educational systems.

On the demand side little is known about the factors which influence the amounts and types of education sought by people. Nor is it known how such demands are in turn linked to the demand and supply of educated manpower in the labour market; so that little of a positive nature can be advanced concerning the economic element in individual motivation for education. Again, there is, if anything, even greater ignorance regarding the economic benefits accruing to the community from the presence of educated people. Not only is there uncertainty as to the nature of such benefits, there is even doubt as to whether they are positive or negative, though the balance of opinion favours the former view.

This almost universal ignorance also extends to the supply side of education. In most cases there is no usable measure or description of the end-product which any given course of study is supposed to produce. There are little or no data on the way in which the quality of the end-product varies as the amount of resources used is increased or decreased. Few attempts have been made to explore the effects which different educational methods have on the product-cost relationship.

The list could be extended, but the examples used are adequate to show that the data which would permit their appraisal in economic terms have been lacking. The absence of any adequate regard to the economic aspects of their activities does not in itself mean that educational systems have been operated in an 'irrational' manner, but is rather a reflection of the behaviour expected of them by educators and public alike.

It would be comparatively easy to explain why this relative neglect of economic aspects should have existed. But to explain is not to justify, and as education expands and absorbs a growing share of community resources, it becomes important to develop systematic procedures to ensure its efficient operation. This need could perhaps be paraphrased in the form that education is too serious a matter to be left in the hands of the educators.

It is also too serious an area to be left in the hands of economists. Increasingly the evidence is that a comprehensive interdisciplinary approach is needed in order to arrive at an adequate understanding of the role and functioning of education. Valuable contributions have come from areas such as psychology, sociology, biochemistry and engineering and it would seem that future progress will continue to require the contributions of many fields of knowledge. The role of economics in this process will not be a trivial one, but following its usual practice its major contributions may be expected to lie in the realm of identifying the relevant questions to be asked, rather than itself providing the answers.

Index